T0157175

Accountability Now!

Accountability Now!

✦

Living the Ten Principles
of Personal Leadership

Mark Sasscer with Maureen McNeill

ACCOUNTABILITY NOW!
Living the Ten Principles of Personal Leadership

iUniverse books may be ordered through booksellers or by contacting:

iUniverse
1663 Liberty Drive
Bloomington, IN 47403
www.iuniverse.com
1-800-Authors (1-800-288-4677)

Because of the dynamic nature of the Internet, any web addresses or links contained in this book may have changed since publication and may no longer be valid. The views expressed in this work are solely those of the author and do not necessarily reflect the views of the publisher, and the publisher hereby disclaims any responsibility for them.

Any people depicted in stock imagery provided by Getty Images are models, and such images are being used for illustrative purposes only. Certain stock imagery © Getty Images.

ISBN: 978-1-4502-1221-2 (sc)
ISBN: 978-1-4502-1220-5 (hc)
ISBN: 978-1-4502-1222-9 (e)

Print information available on the last page.

iUniverse rev. date: 11/22/2018

For my father and mother:
my journey has helped me realize how much you loved me.

Contents

Acknowledgments

This book has been a true pleasure to write because of the partnership that Maureen McNeill and I enjoy. We started working together, confident that I had the content (i.e., the principles, experiences, and research) and that she had the talent to help put my thoughts on paper. In the process of assisting me with my last book and cowriting this one, she has become an ambassador for the Ten Principles, in her life and in her work. I value our professional relationship and the friendship it has inspired.

My wife and three boys (Michael, Sean, and Ryan) live these Ten Principles with me, and I'm grateful for their feedback and perspectives, which support me. My wife, Cheryl, and my son, Sean, were particularly helpful with this book, reviewing drafts and offering their thoughts and ideas.

I'm also grateful to my LeadQuest team, who live these principles every day and help others do the same through workshops and coaching sessions. They are (in alphabetical order):

Dennis Alimena, PhD	Kristin Anderson
Amanda Druckemiller	Elinor Horner
Shari Levy	Andy Milberg
Susan North, ScD	Cheryl Sasscer
Barry Savage	Bill Snavely

Many of the executives with whom I have worked over the years have played an integral role in the development of this book. They took time out of their busy schedules to be interviewed about their experiences with the Ten Principles and offered candid, often enlightening, responses that you'll find quoted here. While their stories are not attributed to them by name (as we agreed in the interview process to respect their privacy), they provide honest illustrations of the Ten Principles in action.

They are (in alphabetical order):

Gina Alteri	Dave Bailey, MD
Joyce Baldrica	Gary Berg, MD
Robert Bridges	Debbie Chang

B. J. Clark, MD

Leslie Crespi

Tom Deutsch, MD

Kelley Dillion

Michael Erhard, MD

Carl Gartner, MD

Jane Hayes

Elliot Joseph

Stephen Lawless, MD

Michele McClelland

David Moser, MD

Gretchen Parker

Diane Radloff

Seth Rosenblatt

Gordon Salm

Steve Sparks

Jo Ann Tuscany

Ernie Yoder

Jeffrey Zaks, MD

Chip Cover

Jay Cummings, MD

Vince Dibattista

Jim Elsner

Tom Ferry

Sr. Betty Granger

Sandy Hess

Michael Kittoe

Craig Livermore

Mary Mehta, MD

Mary Naber

Roy Projansky, MD

Joyce Rapske

Gidget Ruscetta

Bob Scully, MD

Tara Swearingen

Tom Wright

Terri Young

Introduction

We all want happiness. In the United States, we believe its pursuit is a fundamental right. However, as Thomas Paine wrote in December of 1776, "These are the times that try men's souls." Many people in our country would say that this quote describes life today, as we find ourselves in the grasp of the first major recession of the twenty-first century.

In these times, as I travel around the country and speak with leaders from all walks of life, the key question I hear is: "Everyone [customers, employees, their families, etc.] seems to be worried or fearful right now. What more can I do as a leader to help people embrace uncertainty and change so that we don't fall victim to them?"

To help others, leaders must learn how to become even more accountable and resilient themselves. Then, they must model these behaviors for others and teach and coach them on how to do the same. Accountability and resiliency are key ingredients for success and happiness, no matter what the economy or life throws at us.

As the founder and owner of a leadership consulting firm, LeadQuest Consulting, Inc., I work with and coach business leaders every single day who seek to improve themselves and their organizations. They seek to achieve success, to increase their fortunes, and to find greater happiness—personally and professionally. To accomplish this, I tell them that first they must *accept that change is a part of living* and that they are accountable for how they adapt to it.

This book is about learning how to become more accountable and resilient and how to find greater happiness; additionally (for leaders), it is about creating an environment where others can learn to do the same. The underpinning of this work focuses squarely on self-awareness and personal accountability, because one can only control and change oneself. **Accountability is about taking personal ownership; i.e., owning one's choices, decisions, outcomes, and consequences.**

This book is for all types of leaders—business executives, parents, educators, administrators, small business owners, physicians, community organizers, government officials. In the pages ahead, I will share with you what I have been teaching leaders for the past fifteen years. It is worth noting that the majority of the people who are working with the Ten Principles that we will explore in this book tell me that the principles have had a profound impact on their personal lives as well as their professional ones—in other words, they enjoy more fulfilled and happier lives.

The Ten Principles of Personal Leadership provide ways through which you and I can become more accountable and resilient and create greater happiness at home and at work. They are a guide for how to improve ourselves, our relationships (e.g., making them more trusting), and the outcomes we create. They are a powerful tool to use everyday, in every situation, and in every interaction.

The Ten Principles of Personal Leadership offer a new set of road signs. They have not only helped me; they have helped the people and companies with whom I have worked. Some of these companies have even adopted the Ten Principles as the behavioral standards for their organizations.

The Ten Principles of Personal Leadership are interrelated and interdependent. They are presented below in order. They build from one to the next.

1. Be in the moment.
2. Be authentic and humanistic.
3. Volunteer discretionary effort constantly.
4. Model high performance—desired behaviors that drive desired results.
5. Respect and leverage separate realities.
6. Be curious vs. judgmental.
7. Look in the mirror first—be accountable.
8. Have courageous conversations.

9. Provide timely, clear, and specific performance expectations and feedback.
10. Teach, coach, and mentor—spend at least half of your time developing others.

In the first chapter of this book, I will explore a powerful tenet: how one's thinking drives one's behavior. The subsequent chapters will thoroughly explore each of the Ten Principles. In these chapters, I will share the success stories of many of the leaders who have contributed to this body of work; I will also share stories from my personal journey. The purpose for sharing these stories is to bring the Ten Principles to life and to make them real so you can apply them in your own life. In this vein, at the conclusion of each chapter, there will be a series of questions provided to stimulate personal reflection, choice, and application of the Ten Principles.

A word of caution: **This journey is about progress not perfection**. Some of our clients call that the "Eleventh Principle." If you are looking for perfection in yourself, please choose another book. I am and will always be seeking personal growth and happiness.

It is why I live the Ten Principles—to create my own good fortune and success. Let me be clear. I would not be in this place, at this time, writing this book, if it had not been for the Ten Principles. Reading this book and learning to live these Ten Principles will bring you greater success and happiness as well.

Let's start the journey!

Chapter One

Thinking Drives Behavior

. . . .

"A man is but the product of his thoughts; what he thinks, he becomes."

Mahatma Gandhi

"The greatest discovery of my generation is that man can alter his life simply by altering his attitude of mind."

William James

"Progress is impossible without change, and those who cannot change their minds cannot change anything."

George Bernard Shaw

I begin my seminars by asking a simple question: "Who can you control and change?"

Without fail, people answer, "Me."

Then I ask, "How many of you have ever gotten divorced or broken up, because, at the start of the relationship, you thought that you could change the other person, and subsequently, you failed?"

People laugh. A few sheepishly raise their hands. Once, a woman blurted out, "Three times!"

We think that we understand this concept—that we can only change ourselves. Yet even at these seminars, it's clear that we don't. Rather than face our own issues, we remain focused on fixing the other person. Almost without fail, someone will approach me at the break and say, "I'm really glad so-and-so is here. He [or she] really needs this!"

1

I'll say it again. You can only change yourself. **You can only control your reactions and responses to other people and to the situations that arise in your life**. As I write this, the world economy is struggling to recover from a horrific recession. Each of us is choosing how to respond. That response is creating our success, peace of mind, and ultimately, our happiness.

Those who resort to blaming—one administration or another, one financial institution or another—set a trap for themselves. They see themselves as victims of events too large to control, and so they are. They behave as victims, paralyzed by fear and despair, and become unable to perform at their very best, probably making themselves prime candidates for corporate downsizing.

Those who choose a positive attitude, who call on their inner strengths, who nurture a confidence to adapt and thrive, who choose accountability and resilience—whatever the economy or life sends their way—create that future. They carry themselves with confidence. Having rejected fear, they are free to think clearly and make sound decisions. That sure-footedness is apparent to others as well.

The good news here is that this means they can find strength within themselves as they respond. The problems of the world don't go away, but they can choose how they manage the impact on their lives. They can reject victimhood and choose to see themselves as strong. They can become resilient.

Let me begin by giving you an idea of how I got to where I am, to this point in my personal journey.

I was born in 1953 and grew up in row house in Towson, Maryland. My dad, Joe, was a steelworker and my mom, Mildred, was a public school cafeteria cashier. My dad and mom worked extremely hard and instilled a strong work ethic in me. Very early in life, I learned the value of hard work and the need for the income it produced. I always had multiple jobs, starting at age ten, because that was what was expected of me.

Unfortunately, my parents were both worriers who lacked self-confidence. There always seemed to be a black cloud looming overhead. The steel mill might go on strike, and my father would have to find other work. My sweet and quiet mother worried day in and day out about what the neighbors thought of her, because, while my father had graduated from high school, she had not, and she considered that a personal shortcoming. If one of the neighbors happened to not speak to her, my mother was sure that she had done something to offend that person. I can tell you that was never the case; my mother was and still is a saint compared to most people. However, her low self-esteem and constant worrying told her otherwise.

Growing up, I heard, over and over again, "What would the neighbors say?" as the reason for me to not do what I was thinking about doing. It seemed as though we were always afraid of something or someone, and it (or s/he) was right around the corner.

In the late '50s, I started elementary school at the Catholic school down the street from where we lived and was taught by the Sisters of Mercy. What I remember most about those years of being in Catholic school was learning to "fear a forgiving God." That was quite confusing to me. You see, I had bought into the entire doctrine that, if I didn't live an almost perfect life (yes, there was the confessional, but it, too, was a scary place for a small child), I would end up going to this horrible place called Hell. Did I get a good education? You bet, but, like many Catholic school kids of my generation, I paid a price for it.

As a result, I found myself both worrying about the future and often feeling guilty about the past. I had learned those things well from my parents and from my interpretations of what I had been taught in school. My sole moments of happiness occurred in sports—on the pitching mound, when I was striking out batters, or on the football field, throwing or catching touchdown passes.

Until age forty, I heard the same voices over and over in my head, telling me that I wasn't good enough, because I wasn't perfect, and that I would eventually fail. Even my father's mandate that his sons get college educations was based in fear ("I'll break both your arms if you wind up working in that steel mill!"). So, I opted not to do the things I loved, often afraid that someone would see that I wasn't perfect at them. The influence of this fear was so great that, even though I loved football and was very talented at it, I opted to run cross country instead in high school. You see, I'd grown up playing sandlot tackle football and had never worn a full football uniform. I feared being made fun of because I didn't know how to put all the pads on, etc. Rather than ask for help, I decided not to play.

This fear ultimately took on a louder voice; I made decisions I knew were wrong. Having run away from several relationships during my college years, I entered a marriage at age twenty-two, even though I knew it was a mistake. I convinced myself that not going through with the wedding would prove me to be even more of a failure. Needless to say, the marriage was.

At twenty-five, I agreed to marriage counseling, solely because it presented a way out of the marriage. The counselor was the first person to tell me what I've come to understand is **life's fundamental truth: The only person I can change is me.** The only person I can save is me. The only one with the power to resolve my anger—at my parents, at the nuns, at the Catholic Church, at my perceived lack of control over my life—is me.

That revelation came at a pivotal moment. I felt like I had failed everyone I cared about. I was the divorced father of a new baby (a huge stigma in my strict Catholic family) and I was in counseling (a source of embarrassment to my parents). And, despite professional advice to not do it, I made the choice to forge a relationship with my newly born son, even though my ex-wife promised to ruin any relationship that I could ever possibly have with him.

I decided that this new life was one for which I would hold myself accountable. Not to my parents, not to the nuns, but to myself—and, perhaps, for my son.

A new job at the telephone company introduced me to the field of organization development. I began learning more about human behavior and found myself reaching some conclusions. I attended classes around the country, learning about team and organizational dynamics. I completed a program and earned an Organization Development Certificate at the National Training Laboratories (NTL). I also had the good fortune of working with two consulting firms that introduced me to behavioral and cognitive psychology. I will always be grateful to mentors such as Julie Smith, PhD, and Larry Senn, PhD.

From there, I went on to pursue a master's degree in organization development at the American University. By that time (age forty), I had entered a happy, successful marriage, and my wife and I had two more sons. Then, two months before I graduated in 1994, I left the phone company to start LeadQuest Consulting, Inc.

Looking back on my history of worrying and of carrying several jobs at once in search of security, I am still a bit amazed by the leap of faith. As my wife Cheryl says, I had to believe in myself and follow my heart. We had three kids, three dogs, and a mortgage, and my wife believed in me. She still does. It was her faith, perhaps more than mine, that supported taking the leap.

Yet, even owning my own company and doing the work that I loved and believed in, all of those voices of worry and fear still managed to echo. Even with all that I had learned and was teaching, I still held onto the fear and anger.

Then, one day it dawned on me—my father and mother's behaviors had made sense to them; they truly were doing the best they could with what they knew, understood, and believed. They had had different realities than I had. So had the nuns. Sister Mary Boniface, by whom I felt terrorized in first grade, believed that creating fear was the only way to control and teach young children. My father believed that telling me I was stupid was what a father did to build the toughness I'd need as a man. Their beliefs had driven their behaviors.

They had spoken their truths, their realities.

That realization was liberating for me. Once I understood that my parents had been guided by their beliefs, I was free to choose my own beliefs, my own path. It became clear that **my happiness was mine to choose.**

As you gathered from the stories above, I was a blamer. I blamed my parents, the nuns, the Catholic school, and a host of others for my unhappiness growing up. I've learned since then that I cannot create good fortune by blaming other people for what happened or happens in my life. I can only change myself and my reactions.

If I enter into a relationship with you, planning to change you, I must believe that something about you needs changing, that something about you is not good enough. My ego, my separation from and placement above you in my mind, drives this judgmental attitude, whether or not I am aware of it. Or, put another way: **My relationship with you can only be as good as the conversation I have about you in my mind.**

Rather than taking the proactive and productive approach of changing myself, I become frustrated in the losing (and, to you, insulting) battle of trying to change you. I set up a self-fulfilling prophecy that predicts failure. I treat you badly. You respond in like fashion. My undesired behavior becomes justified in my mind. The prophecy becomes reality.

You can only change you. If you spend most of your energy in life focused on that truth, including how you respond to people and situations that show up in your life, you will ease your journey. You will find your way to happiness by looking in the mirror.

Hand-in-hand with this is the concept that "my thinking drives my behavior." Each of us has formed beliefs or habits of thought over our lifetimes that we hold onto—sometimes with a death grip! These beliefs act as a filter through which we interpret the events that occur in our lives. Some of these beliefs still serve us well. However, there are others that we should shed, for our own good and the good of those around us. Think of the opportunities we miss when we hold onto beliefs that no longer serve us, when we let what Alcoholics Anonymous calls "stinking thinking" drive our behavior. These thoughts are the true seeds of sadness.

In my own life, it has taken me years to learn to believe in myself. My father's idea of preparing me for the demands of manhood was to "toughen" me with his own harsh assessment of me. In the past, my negative thoughts about myself drove my behaviors and even my decisions. In one case, I let self-doubt and fear drive away what would have been a wonderful career opportunity.

About twenty years ago, when I was working for the phone company, I was responsible for bringing in and coordinating the efforts of a small, but highly regarded, consulting firm, which had been hired to build management skills. The lead partner of the firm and I worked together for three years. I came to know and admire the work she did, as well as the work of the professionals on her team, most of whom had doctorates in the science of applied behavior analysis.

As their work was winding down, she approached me one day with a proposal. She told me that she had been talking with her partners and that they had agreed that I had talents they could use. They had concluded that if I joined them as a partner, the firm would be even stronger.

I was stunned. My first response, rather than pride in this compliment or thrill in the potential challenge, was fear. In fact, my answer was a question, "What would your team think? Isn't this unfair to them?"

Let's be clear. My first impulse was not concern for the well-being of her consulting firm. It was fear that I was unworthy of the chance. As much as I believed in this woman and her firm and had learned to trust the value of their work, I chose to hold on to my old belief that I wasn't good enough. I listened more closely to the echo of my father's voice telling me that I didn't deserve success. I allowed myself to be paralyzed by fear.

Incidentally, my instincts about the high caliber of the firm were sound. Four years later, it was bought by a national consulting group for millions of dollars.

What this revealed to me was the fact that I had deep-seeded beliefs, learned in childhood and, on a conscious level, rejected as an adult, which continued to govern my adult behavior. The "aha" for me was that one's self-image is really about one's beliefs. Each of us has beliefs that have been shaped by what we have seen modeled, by what we have been taught, and by what we have had reinforced in us over our lifetimes.

I am very clear that my actions make sense to me. What I need to remember is that **your actions make sense to you.** None of us starts the day looking for ways to be hurtful. Yet, we can spend our days interpreting and judging others' actions as inappropriate or wrong. When we remember that each of us acts according to our own beliefs, we open ourselves up to greater understanding and acceptance of others. This concept of separate realities is the basis for Principle Five. We'll return to it later.

Until I learned to hold myself accountable for my choices, I was unaware that my beliefs were so deeply entrenched, far below the surface, that they had been driving my behavior without me even noticing them. The analogy that works for me is the iceberg. When you look at an iceberg, as enormous as it might seem on the surface, you are only seeing about 20 percent of it. Typically, 80 percent of an iceberg's total mass is below the surface, unseen.

Beliefs are like that. They often lie so deep in our unconsciousness that we carry them around without even acknowledging that they exist. It's what I don't see that can be deadly when it comes to the relationship I have with myself, as well as the relationships I have with others. My behavioral habits, the way I treat myself and others, and even the way I think about the people in my life, are driven by my beliefs. As good relationships are key to my well-being, to my ability to adapt and thrive (my resilience), it's important to become aware of my beliefs and their impact.

Some of us have reached, either by example or from experience, a fundamental belief about the nature of life that drives our behavior—positive or negative. You head out the door in the morning to find a flat tire. For one person, the internal dialogue that begins sees the tire as a portent of doom—"What else can go wrong? This is going to be a miserable day; I can tell already." Another person will manage to take it in stride. S/he changes the tire or calls for help, regarding this either with amusement or, once it's resolved, as a hurdle cleared, and gets on with the day.

Imagine each of these people for a moment. See them in your mind. Look at the expressions on their faces. Which will begin the day with more stress? How will that day play out? How will they treat the people whose paths they cross and how will those people respond? That underlying perspective, that fundamental belief about the positive or negative nature of living, is a matter of choice.

Think about your own life and perspective. If you had to put a percentage on the number of things that are working well in your professional and personal life combined, what would it be? For most of us—and I've asked this question of hundreds of executives over the years—the answer is at least 80 percent. In fact, many have said that 90–95 percent of the things in their lives were working well. Yet where do we focus our energy, whether at work or at home? Many of us target the small percentage of things that are not going well, typically to the exclusion of the other 80 percent or more. We see that flat tire and forget that it's been years since we've had to change one.

When we choose this focus, we choose a belief that then drives our behavior.

I propose an alternative. Rather than punishing yourself with a quest for perfection, look at the big picture. Celebrate and leverage the 80 percent of your life that is working well while you address the 20 percent that could be working even better. This is vitally important for personal, team, and organizational (or family) health and success. When we focus exclusively on the small number of things that aren't going well, we become driven by negativity and fear. When we focus on what is going well, we are driven by confidence. We are open to learning from the successes to improve the things that need improvement.

In this vein, responding to others based on a particular focus has consequences. Author Richard Carlson, PhD, described the phenomenon of "operating on autopilot." When you are on autopilot, you react out of habit, often unconsciously. For example, imagine that you are standing in the ticket line at a movie theater when, all of a sudden, you are pushed forcefully from behind. Automatically, without thinking, you turn around and angrily say, "Watch it!" The words have left your mouth before you've even seen the face of the person standing behind you. This conditioned reaction occurs automatically and instantaneously. When you do make eye contact with the person behind you, you discover a deeply apologetic elderly man who simply lost his balance and fell forward. Would you have chosen a different response (to the stimulus of being bumped), if you had paused, assumed the best, and turned to see what had happened before responding? Choosing to turn off autopilot by pausing can produce better relationships, outcomes, and greater happiness.

It should not be surprising that operating on autopilot can literally be harmful. For example, you are driving on a road that you've traveled down many times before, and you are daydreaming. You stop at the intersection and then head across it, when all of a sudden, a car comes careening down the road straight for you. Your reaction time is slow, and you can't avoid the impact. One minute you're lost in thought; the next, you're T-boned.

Autopilot behavior can have a negative impact on relationships too. Remember that "my relationship with you can only be as good as the conversation I have about you in my mind." Suppose we work together, and you are delivering a presentation at a meeting. If the conversation I have about you in my mind puts us in competition with one another, I begin acting on autopilot, looking for something in your presentation with which to disagree. Without thinking about my behavior, I begin squirming in my seat or, even worse, rolling my eyes. I communicate my beliefs to you and perhaps others without even realizing it. I may not intend to be disrespectful, but that is the impact of my behavior.

If I understand that beliefs drive behaviors and that many of these beliefs live so deep within me that they are unconscious and unavailable to me in the moment, the key question is "How do I take control of my behavior?"

The first step is **awareness**. Being self-aware means recognizing when I am on autopilot and seeing the impact of my behavior on those around me. More than that, it is becoming aware of my thinking and how it influences my behavior. My feelings, my emotions, are reflections of my thoughts. To increase self-awareness, I need to pause when there is something I'm feeling and then connect that feeling—whether it is happiness or fear or frustration—to what is producing it in my mind. Once I've recognized the connection between emotion and thought, I can look for and examine the underlying beliefs that have been driving my thinking. For example, growing up, my belief (i.e., thought habit) that I was not good enough caused me to feel jealous and/or angry toward others, which then showed up in my behavior; needless to say, the impact of my behavior on others was often hurtful.

The second step in controlling behavior is to use another powerful action before reacting—**pausing before reacting** (this may be counting to ten before responding to someone). Since my feelings act as a barometer that indicates my state of mind, I can become more attuned to its reading—stormy or calm thoughts. I can take time to pause and reflect on the thinking that is driving my feelings and creating my mood.

The third step is to **consciously choose an appropriate response.** In that moment of self-reflection, I can decide if my truth—what I'm thinking—is the absolute truth; would what I see as the truth be accepted by everyone else in the same situation as the truth?

If you are presenting at a meeting and I find myself getting annoyed at you, I need to pause and get in touch with the health of my own thinking about you. I can determine if it's productive in that setting and then choose the appropriate behavior and responses during your presentation. I don't have to like you to respect you and listen to what you have to say. In fact, if I dislike you, on deeper reflection, I'll probably find that I can learn something about myself and my reactions from that experience.

In my leadership work, the model I've developed for these three steps is *Awareness→Reflection→Choice* (ARC). For us to create happiness and success, we must become more aware of our beliefs and behaviors and their impact. Are my beliefs truly valid? Are my behaviors, informed and driven by those beliefs, serving me well? Is the impact that I have the one that I intend and desire? I have a choice about each of these.

To make the choice, I need to understand that the thought that I hold about you is just that—a thought. Thinking is involuntary; it is happening all of the time. When I am aware of the health of my thinking and its impact, I can change my thinking and, as a result, my behavior.

Each of my thoughts carries no real weight unless I want it to. My thinking about people and situations is something that I've created, albeit out of habit, and, therefore, something that is within my control. I can build new habits of thought. When I become aware of a thought habit, I can ask myself, "Is this serving me well in this moment?" If I attend a meeting to learn from a presentation, is hostility my best choice? Wouldn't I be better served by setting aside judgment and opening up to your presentation?

ARC gives me the opportunity to shape not only my response but even the thought behind it. To understand this better, let's go back to my blaming behavior. For years, when something would go wrong or when I'd feel that I had failed, I'd automatically hear my father's voice and remember him calling me stupid. This opened the door to a downward spiral of defensiveness, anger, and frustration. I had internalized his message that I was not good enough and had woven it into my own thought process.

The power of ARC is in the opportunity to redirect that process. I can reflect and change my response to a familiar trigger. I recognize that **I can control my thoughts and can choose a positive attitude that will serve me well.** I can even change the way I think about my father. When I acknowledge that my father thought that he was doing the right thing, that he thought he was preparing me to be strong for whatever life had to offer, I can let go of the anger. I can turn off his voice in my head and learn to prevent an unhealthy response. When I pause to reflect, I see that I have the power to choose my response. I can choose forgiveness and happiness.

Eleanor Roosevelt said it best: "No one can make you feel inferior without your consent."

If happiness has its roots in luck, my happiness comes from choosing to think of myself as fortunate. My positive attitude and thoughts will drive my behavior. I have the power to choose. I can choose to be happy.

"Happiness is the meaning and the purpose of life, the whole aim and end of human existence." —Aristotle

Chapter One Review: Thinking drives behavior.

- You cannot control others; you can only control yourself, your reactions, and your responses.
- Your mental attitude creates your reality.
- Your relationship with others can only be as good as the conversation you have about them in your mind.
- Your beliefs (i.e., thought habits) drive your behavior.
- Beliefs are like icebergs: 20 percent shows; 80 percent is hidden.
- Just as your behavior makes sense to you, others' behavior makes sense to them.
- There are three steps to changing behavior: awareness, reflection, and choice (ARC).
- Being self-aware means recognizing when you are on autopilot and seeing the impact of your behavior on those around you.
- Choosing to turn off autopilot by *pausing* can produce better relationships, outcomes, and greater happiness.

In the next chapter, we'll build further on these concepts and explore Principle One: Be in the moment.

Thinking Drives Behavior: Personal Reflection

To help you experience these principles in action, each chapter will have a section designed to help you apply them in your daily life. By answering the questions and reflecting on your answers, you will gain insight into how making different choices will benefit you.

For this chapter, think of one interaction (with a coworker, your boss, your spouse/partner, or your child) that occurred this week that you believe went poorly and examine it closely.

1. What happened? How did you behave? How did the other person respond to your behavior? Did you get the outcome(s) you wanted? How did that feel?

_____

_____

_____

_____

2. Did you react without thinking, or did you carefully choose your actions? If you had paused to reflect and choose a more appropriate response, how might you have behaved differently? How might the outcome(s) have been more favorable for both parties?

_____

_____

_____

_____

3. What kind of thinking was behind your actions? What beliefs about yourself and/or about the other person led you to behave the way you did?

_____

_____

_____

_____

4. Do you know for a fact that those beliefs were true? Did they serve you well in that interaction? Are they worth holding onto?

_____

_____

_____

_____

5. What will you do next time to remind yourself to pause, reflect, and choose—to take yourself off autopilot (e.g., recognize your feelings and count to ten before responding)?

_____

_____

_____

_____

6. What beliefs will you choose that will support a positive view of yourself and the other person? How will this benefit you and the relationship that you have with the other person? How will the outcomes you achieve together be even better?

_____

_____

_____

_____

Be accountable now!

Chapter Two

Principle One: Be in the Moment

. . . .

"Life is not lost by dying; life is lost minute by minute, day by day, in all the thousand, small, uncaring ways."

Stephen Saint Vincent Benet

"Life is what happens while you are making other plans."

John Lennon

When my oldest of three sons turned thirty-one last year, I said over and over again to friends and business colleagues what people often say, "Where did the years go?" Sometimes I heard sadness in my voice; the implication being that, with better choices, those years could have been happier. The question I pondered was, "Had I chosen to be more present, to be more in the moment, where might the years have taken us?"

I asked the question, because I had been thinking about the answer. Following the example of my mother, I had spent much of my son's lifetime living in either the past or the future. I blamed myself for divorcing his mother and not being more present in his life. I worried about where I'd find the money for his college education. I doubted that we would be able to have a good relationship, that I'd be a better parent than my own dad. I spent much of that time feeling guilty about the past and worrying about what was coming (or not coming).

It has only been in recent years that I have learned to and been able to cherish the special moments I have with my family, even if we're all just watching television together. In those moments, my wife, my three sons and their significant others, and our basset hounds simply enjoy one another's company.

I recently overheard someone telling his friend, "I'm taking vacation in three months, and I can't wait! I'm counting the days." It appears that he is unhappy in this moment, perhaps with his job, but think of the time he is losing by focusing on the future rather than living for today. Think of the opportunities for happiness that he is putting off for those ninety days.

When we are born, each of us should be given one of those colorful wristbands. The one I'm suggesting would say, "Happiness is found in *this* moment." That's the message that should be reinforced over and over again as we learn and grow. For me—and this is why it's Principle One of the Ten Principles of Personal Leadership—it's the foundation upon which everything else builds. **Being in the moment is about being fully present (mentally, emotionally, and spiritually) for, as well as physically engaged in, what's happening right now**. It is nothing less than the key that unlocks the door to happiness!

When I am in that place, when I am mentally and emotionally connected to everything that is happening, I am able to fully see and experience the beauty in things. I hear things that I normally cannot hear. I see the greenness of the lawn and the beauty of each shade of green. What's even more powerful is that I am able to see what is good and wonderful in this world, rather than allowing the negative messages that are projected by the TV or radio to simply wash over me. My thinking, and hence my behavior, is shaped by what is good around me rather than by negative or noisy distractions.

Even if I am in an environment that is not so beautiful—for example, if I am heading for one more meeting at work where we'll learn about budget cuts—being in the moment gives me access to my best thinking. I am reminded of my strengths. I approach the meeting with confidence in my ability to contribute positively to the discussion and outcome. When I am in the moment and fully aware, I am able to adapt and be resilient.

On the other hand, when faced with change and adversity, some people focus on the past. They look back on choices they've made or chances that have passed them by and become mired in regret. That choice to harness themselves to the past determines how they will weather the current storm. Only if I am in the moment am I free to be my best self. I accept that change happens, confident that I can adapt to it. I am resilient in the face of adversity, because I believe that "this, too, shall pass." My positive outlook is found in each moment, in each choice. My thinking drives my behavior and has the power to carry me through the storm. Henry Ford explained this well: "Think you can, think you can't; either way, you'll be right."

It's no coincidence that my best moments as a child were on the playing field, and today, they are in my seminars and coaching sessions. There is a saying from one of my heroes that captures this. Football great John Brody said, "A player's effectiveness is directly related to his ability to be right there, doing that thing, in the moment … he can't be worrying about the past or the future or the crowd or some other extraneous event. He must be able to respond in the here and now." In my seminars, I am totally in the moment and fully aware. I have to be and want to be.

When I am completely in the moment, I am focused, attuned to what's going on around me. I am aware of subtle changes in facial expressions and body language. I listen for the slight shift in tone of voice that tells me that a thought is ready to be expressed. I am in the zone, and I am truly happy. I can draw on the wisdom that is in me—and in the group—and bring it forward. The wisdom is in each of us, ready to be drawn out. Being in the moment is the door opener. We can then choose to step through. When we choose to take that step, we can communicate with one another in a new, deeper, and more meaningful way. We hear each other as if for the first time, because we are all truly engaged. It's a beautiful thing.

Each of us—including each of the executives in my seminars—has the wisdom to make choices that will lead to greater success and happiness. When we are all in the moment, we can draw on that wisdom. In truth, the executives don't really need a consultant like me. Each of us can communicate at a deeper and richer level, at which we not only listen to one another but truly hear and understand what is being said. When we are in the moment, the quality of what we do and the efficiency with which we produce it goes way up.

Pat, a high-level executive at a client company, has begun reaping the benefits of being in the moment. Here's how Pat describes it: "What I've learned to appreciate is that, by focusing all of my attention and energy on performing one task at a time, I am able to be far more efficient and effective. When I take the time to do one thing really well, even if it's a personal thing versus a work thing, all of the other pieces seem to fall into place—for a variety of reasons. Now, people find that when they get their turn with me, they feel well attended to, and I feel like I'm doing a good job. I've come to realize that multitasking is a bit of smoke and mirrors."

In my seminars, when I am in the moment and my ego is disengaged, I'm able to recognize the goodness at the core of even the harshest and most cynical of the high-powered executives with whom I work. I am able to see the good in them and realize that they are generally unaware of the impact of the intimidating exteriors that they project. Their behavior makes sense to them. They have successfully climbed the corporate ladder exhibiting that behavior, so it has been reinforced over the years in very powerful ways. **When I am in the moment, I can be curious enough to see who they are without judging them.** I recognize learned behavior. Only when I am in the moment, can I truly choose curiosity. (This concept—choosing curiosity over judgment—is one of the Ten Principles, which we'll come to in a later chapter.)

The reverse is equally true. **When I am not in the moment, I often find myself going through life on autopilot**—falling into my old cognitive and behavioral habits without even being conscious of them and their impact.

Since I travel so much, it has become my routine, after a long day of work, to go out to dinner. If I'm on autopilot, I revert to my old, bad eating habits. I go for the high-carb, high-fat comfort foods that I remember from my youth and in the quantities that I enjoyed at my mother's table. I'm not making conscious choices about what's best for me or even about what I'd enjoy most. And that is why I continue to struggle with my weight.

Then I go back to my hotel room, catch up on e-mail and voicemail, and then turn on the television and either doze off in front of it or find a show that I enjoy. Sometimes the phone will ring, and I'll answer it, but because I've already shut down for the night, I'm in a hurry to get off the phone. I'm not fully present for the person calling. I participate in the discussion—I'm polite; I respond—but I am not truly attentive to our conversation. I would be better off accepting my choice to watch TV and agreeing to return the call later. When I am on autopilot, I answer the phone out of habit and engage without being fully present. The lesson here is that, if I can't be in the moment for someone else, out of respect for them and myself, I need to say that to them and schedule another time to talk.

Without greater self-awareness, you may make negative choices, and these behaviors can become routines that impact your personal health and relationships. Here, I have another choice—I can expect perfection of myself and return to my cycle of thinking that I'm not good enough and turn to blaming behavior, or I can remember that I am making progress. I am aware of my actions and on a path to choosing better ones.

The voice in my mind can be a powerful force, especially if I consider the influence of self-fulfilling prophecies. If I tell myself that I am a miserable, hopeless failure, this "self-talk" will lead to a sour mood. That will be borne out in my facial expressions and the way I participate in conversations. My belief will drive my behavior. My behavior will likely influence the way others perceive me and behave toward me. Their behavior supports or reinforces the thinking that began the cycle—that I am a hopeless failure.

If, on the other hand, I tell myself I am fortunate and can achieve whatever I put my mind to, that prophecy has its own power. I believe in my good fortune. My positive outlook is visible not only in my actions but also in my expressions and even in my demeanor.

With greater self-awareness, you can make positive choices when you are aware of what you are doing and its impact. This requires that you take time to understand why you do what you do. When you are in the moment, you can choose to make a change for the better.

Angela is the vice president of human resources for one of our client companies. She has found that being in the moment has had a powerful impact on her leadership.

"I always thought that I was in the moment, because I'm a pretty good listener and when people come to see me, I'm not doing other things. I'm really paying attention to them. But, what I didn't realize was that being in moment really meant investing time (quiet time) in planning ahead, not doing too many things by the seat of my pants, and being a lot more intentional about what I say, how I say it, and when I say it.

"For me, it is really about getting in touch with how I'm responding—and really being in that moment when I'm responding. In holding people accountable, have I given them specific expectations and confirmed that they understand those expectations? Am I attending to that? Am I following up with feedback? All of that is really about being in the moment. That's where the power comes from!"

How can you become aware that you are not in the moment? It requires practice. In my seminars, at different times during the day, I ask people to share what they've learned or relearned about themselves and what they'll choose to do differently going forward. What often happens is that, after people begin sharing—and this can be a fantastic, rich thing—I'll pause and ask, "How many of you truly heard what was being said and how it was being said, rather than thinking about what you'll say when it's your turn?" The moment the conversation begins in my head about what I am going to say or my critique of what you are saying, I am no longer in the moment. It's an easy and common mistake to make, but making it means missing the meaning, the intention, the real benefit of the exercise, of the group sharing. It means missing not only what others have said but also what you might have learned from how they said it, their nonverbal communication. Human interactions and communication are enhanced when we choose to "just be"—to fully be in the moment for the other person(s). When we fail to make this choice, our mental distractions often lead to misinterpretations and misunderstandings, which can damage relationships.

If you want to change, one important technique is to measure your progress. There is an old saying that "we measure what we treasure." Measuring helps us become more aware of our behavior, especially behavior that we want to improve. For example, for the principle of being in the moment, the simplest way would be to keep track of your interactions during the day, marking on your calendar "Y" for yes or "N" for no at the conclusion of each interaction. The "Y" or "N" would indicate whether you were in the moment during that interaction. At the end of the day, you can see how you've done. You can even determine the percentage of the time that you were in the moment that day. Within a few days, you should start seeing trends. Remember that this is a tool for making progress. Don't expect perfection from yourself.

Measuring helps me identify and analyze my patterns of behavior. If there are certain people with whom I find it difficult to be in the moment, I have the opportunity to ask myself why. What am I thinking or believing about those people that is influencing my behavior and taking me out of the moment?

Going back to the sharing exercise mentioned above, the reason people are not in the moment is often related to ego. They want to make sure that what they say is viewed positively; it might be that they want what they say to be as good as or better than what someone else said. They are focused not on what is happening in the moment but on their upcoming performance.

Let's be clear; ego is the self seeing itself as separate and distinct from the world and others. Egocentric people see themselves as being "the center of the universe." Their perception is that everything should revolve around and satisfy them. The humanistic person, on the other hand, sees himself/herself in the context of the world and others. The humanistic person is often selfless; s/he is more self-aware than the egocentric person when it comes to understanding the impact of his/her behavior on other people and on relationships. More importantly, the humanistic person truly cares about the impact s/he has on others and demonstrates that through respectful and kind behavior. (In the next chapter, we will explore in more detail what it means to be humanistic.)

Being in the moment requires self-awareness and respect for other human beings. There is plenty of room in the world for ego, uniqueness, and individuality. But, when I value my ego more highly than my relationships, when I feel I have to prove my worth to you at your expense, we both lose.

One final point about being in the moment and being on autopilot: I've noticed that I am most often on (negative) autopilot behavior with those to whom I am closest—for example, my wife. I think one key factor here is learned behavior. My own parents were rarely affectionate with one another in my presence. So the example I learned from was a household dominated by a distant and critical father. Turning my time and attention to my wife and family requires intentionality. When I am in the moment and have turned off autopilot, I choose different, healthier behaviors with my family. Turning off autopilot requires me to be self-aware so that I can push the "pause button" and choose desired behavior.

When I talk to my clients, I find we often have this in common. Elaine is the vice president of a large corporation and the single mother of two teenage boys. She has come to realize the importance of being in the moment at home in building stronger relationships with her sons. "They need to know I am present and available to them and that I care about what is going on in their lives," she told me. "I now take more time to be in the moment, to make sure that we have quality time together and that I am giving them appreciative feedback so they don't just hear 'what's this mess in the kitchen?' and so on. They know I appreciate the good choices they make too."

Being in the moment provides the focus that we need to maintain the relationships that matter most to us. Those who know and care for us notice the difference. Even in more casual relationships—in community organizations, in church groups, and at work—being in the moment provides the perspective we need to communicate openly, honestly, and clearly. This provides the foundation for working well together and forging healthy relationships.

Principle One Review: Be in the moment.

- Being in the moment means being fully present and engaged (mentally and emotionally) in what's happening right now—not the past, not the future.
- Being in the moment allows you to experience others in a more complete way (i.e., being more attuned to their verbal and non-verbal communications and the feelings behind them).
- Not being in the moment may result in negative autopilot behavior that results in negative choices; these choices can have an undesired impact on relationships.
- Positive choices come from self–awareness; you become more self-aware when you are in the moment, because you are more conscious of what is occurring.
- You can measure progress for in-the-moment behavior by tracking it daily.
- Being in the moment improves all relationships—business, personal, and spiritual.

The next chapter will focus on Principle Two: Be authentic and humanistic. This will build on the concepts from Principle One (Be in the moment) that you learned in this chapter.

BE IN THE MOMENT: PERSONAL REFLECTION

Think of a time when you were at your best. You were engrossed in a task that you loved, and you were doing your very best work.

1. Describe the moment: the sights and sounds and your thoughts, feelings, and behaviors.

    _____

    _____

    _____

    _____

2. What kept distractions at bay? How did you maintain focus? What kept you in *that* moment?

    _____

    _____

    _____

    _____

3. What were you able to achieve by being totally in that moment?

    _____

    _____

    _____

    _____

4. How did it feel to succeed?

    _____

    _____

    _____

    _____

5. In your daily life, how often can you summon that focus? What percentage of the time are you fully in the moment for what you are doing?

    _____

    _____

    _____

    _____

6. What will you do to remind yourself to stay fully present? How will you let go of old habits and beliefs (e.g., reliving regrets from the past or being impatient for the future) that get in the way of you remaining in the moment?

    _____

    _____

    _____

    _____

7. What will you achieve when you are in the moment for more of your life? How will this impact your happiness?

    _____

    _____

    _____

    _____

Be accountable now!

Chapter Three

Principle Two: Be Authentic and Humanistic

. . . .

"Be who you are. This is the first step toward becoming better than you are."

Julius Charles Hare

"It is true that, in all communication, kindness without honesty is sentimentality; but it is likewise true that honesty without kindness is cruelty. The genius of communication is the ability to be both totally honest and totally kind at the same time."

John Powell

As a college student, I enrolled in a religion course and then found out that most of my classmates were ministers, priests, and nuns! From the first day, I was certain they knew the material better than I did. That wasn't a big problem until I was required to make a presentation for the class about a passage from the Old Testament.

Wanting to do my best, I researched the presentation well. I worked hard and was anxious to succeed. The instructor, perhaps anticipating my anxiety, scheduled my presentation among the last in the class. Even with the extra time, when I stood up to speak, I found myself looking out at a sea of experts on the subject. The voice in my head, sounding like my father's, told me that I was stupid and could never say anything that they'd find useful. On top of that, memories of Catholic school and the criticism I'd received from nuns flooded my mind. I had prepared more for that presentation than for any other in my career as a student, but I was overcome with the fear that nothing I did would be good enough.

I decided to open up to the class—to be totally honest and vulnerable. I started out telling them how much I was dreading the presentation and about who they represented for me in my life. I shared with them my fear that they would judge me harshly. What I saw in their eyes was empathy. So much so that the thought came to me: "We are all equal in God's eyes." Suddenly, I was able to let go of my fear, to be myself, and to draw on both my hours of research and my own perspective and wisdom. I delivered a presentation that touched them in a very powerful way.

Besides empathy, what I saw in my college classmates was their humanity; I truly believed that they wanted me to be successful. That enabled me to be authentic and humanistic with them. By putting the situation into its proper perspective—that we were all students in the class together and we all had something to learn and something to offer one another—I was able to draw on my own strengths and to bolster my resilience and do well.

Being authentic means being your true self, genuine and honest. Being humanistic is being respectful of others and treating them the way that they would like to be treated. This is different from the Golden Rule, which tells us to treat others the way we want to be treated. This is about respecting individuality. (We'll spend more time on individual or separate realities in chapter six.) When I remind myself that my way isn't the only way, when I take the time to consider the feelings of the person with whom I'm talking, I am prepared to be completely candid without doing harm.

The two words that make up Principle Two, "authentic" and "humanistic," are paired for a very specific and meaningful reason. In my work, I find that some people misinterpret being authentic (or being honest) to mean that they can speak their truths without regard for how the other person may receive the message or the impact that it might have on his/her self-esteem. **When I pair being humanistic with being authentic, I stress the importance of not only *what* is said, but *how* it is said.**

This goes back to the fact that one's behavior makes sense to him/her. Being humanistic is about putting yourself in the other person's shoes and caring enough to try to understand him/her. Just as important as being honest with him/her is being mindful of his/her feelings.

When I was growing up, I learned a very powerful belief. I'm sure many of us heard it recited to us. "If you can't say something nice, don't say anything at all." Since my thinking drove my behavior, it should not come as a surprise that I often avoided saying anything negative, even if I believed it could be helpful. I chose not to share my thoughts, because I believed it wouldn't be "nice" to do so. I actively and carefully avoided conflict.

This belief was reinforced not only in Catholic school but also by my mother, who was afraid of saying anything that might be interpreted as being the least bit negative. My mother lived in constant fear of hurting someone's feelings. The fear paralyzed her. To this day, when we head to a family gathering, she will say to me, "Now, don't bring this up, and don't say that, because they might take it the wrong way." I tease her, saying how amazing it is that I can function and even succeed when she isn't around to guide my actions 24/7.

Before I learned to deflect conflict and criticism with humor, I struggled with it. In steering clear of conflict, I was denying my true self, my real feelings. As a consequence, I would become angry and frustrated. One source of my anger and frustration was the obvious willingness of others to ignore the rules and to say things to me that were far from nice. After all, my father seemed to have no problem calling me "stupid," not once but with regularity. Did this power, this willingness to hurt others come with age or with authority?

My response was to rebel. I was fighting for respect—my father's and my own. I struggled to find my authentic self. I bounced from one extreme to the other. I was blunt and hurtful in responding to my college girlfriend. I became defensive when a coworker challenged my opinions or tried to help me.

The problem with the "Don't say anything at all" rule is that it nurtures dishonesty. Raised to abide by it, I spent years not speaking up. Rather than saying what I needed to say, I let frustration and anger build inside of me rather than being genuine with people. I know I am not alone in this. Only recently, I read a letter to Miss Manners from a man who had allowed a party hostess to call him by the wrong name over and over again during the course of an evening—even introducing him to others by the wrong name—rather than risk offending her by correcting her.

Following this rule also inspires us to suppress information. After all, its corollary is "What you don't know can't hurt you." Neither of these rules is actually helpful. They may come from a desire to be kind, but they don't always wind up that way. Intention does not equal impact.

My father believed what he'd learned from his father: "Spare the rod, spoil the child." Letting me or my brother become "spoiled" would not only harm us, but it would reflect badly on him. In his mind, he even took into account our individuality. I have one sibling, a brother. In our home, the belief was that my brother had the brains, and I had the personality and athleticism. This was the belief, so it took on its own reality, irrespective of the facts.

He decided that my future career would be in baseball. As a talented baseball player himself when he was young, his goal for me was that I become a professional baseball player. I was a hard-throwing pitcher who threw strikes; in my father's eyes, that made baseball my job. As a consequence, our only relationship revolved around baseball. The only approval I got from him—the person I needed to please the most, whose approval I valued above all others, including my own—came from playing baseball. Fortunately, I was a very good pitcher.

At the end of each season, like clockwork, I was chosen to play in the annual all-star game. Our standings secure, this was the one game during the entire season that, in my opinion, was played just for fun. For several years, I pitched in the annual game. In my eighth all-star year, I decided to have more fun than usual. I joked around and even began telling the batters what type of pitch (e.g., fastball, curve, or slider) I was about to deliver.

My father saw this and took it to mean that I was failing to take baseball seriously. At the end of the game, he was furious with me. He told me I had embarrassed myself and him. My goofing off on the pitcher's mound meant that I didn't play the game passionately enough. He told me that I'd never amount to anything as a baseball player, and he added that he wasn't sure that I'd amount to anything in life. Then he delivered his final salvo: He swore he'd never come to watch me play baseball again. Since I had been five years old, he had watched every game I had ever played—then it was over. The only bond I had ever known with him had come to an abrupt end.

Telling someone—especially your son or daughter—that s/he is not good enough is among the most powerful forces of nature. Now, I understand that my father was simply speaking his truth. He was being authentic. He was not, however, being humanistic. It was not in his frame of reference as a father to take my feelings into consideration.

As a consequence, his proclamation became a self-fulfilling prophecy. When the next season began, I took the mound on opening day and looked for my dad in the stands. True to his word, he was nowhere to be found. I played a terrible game. I couldn't throw a strike to save my life. On some level, I believed that I was worthless without him. I felt badly about myself, and I blamed him. I never played baseball again after that season.

The messages we convey to our children are powerful—not only the things we say but also (and more importantly) the things we do. The principle—be authentic and humanistic—is valuable in all relationships. I believe it is central to being a loving parent. In fact, the old saw, "Do as I say, not as I do," is a message that packs a punch. My father called me stupid but punished me severely if I was disrespectful. Combine that with my mother's model of fearing conflict, and it created intense confusion. It can produce a downward spiral in which any sense of self is lost.

Being a parent requires being authentic, and it always requires being humanistic and respectful of our children. Consider the power of telling our children that our love for them is unconditional. That knowledge, provided our behavior proves it to be true, frees them to have confidence in their own identities. It plants the seeds of strength that will grow and serve them in the face of adversity. It also teaches them how trust is formed and strengthened.

If our children see that there are consequences—positive and negative—of their actions, they learn from those consequences. If I've asked my son to cut the grass and then tell him how much I sincerely appreciate it when he completes the task well, he sees that it matters to me, and he feels good about completing the work. If he cuts the grass and the next thing I say is, "Why is your room such a mess, mister?," he learns that I can't be pleased. He learns that my word cannot be trusted.

As leaders in settings such as the workplace, we have a responsibility to ourselves and to those on our team to be both authentic and humanistic. Consequences continue to be important. If we supervise a team and set expectations, those expectations are communicated not just in job descriptions but in our day-to-day communication. It is another way of demonstrating that we are invested in the team's success.

Being an authentic and humanistic leader can bring tremendous rewards. Humanistic leaders, who are good listeners and demonstrate empathy, benefit by building trusting relationships that nurture resilience in times of change or difficulty. That doesn't mean it doesn't seem risky at first. One of my clients, Eric, the CEO of a multi-company organization, pointed out to me that humanistic leadership has, inherent in it, a measure of vulnerability—something he initially feared and now considers a benefit.

Having been raised in an era that favored stoicism, Eric was surprised to find that any of the Ten Principles—and particularly ones that open the leader up to being vulnerable—can be successful for him. And yet his experience has proven that it can be and is.

"Authentically exposing your inner self, exposing your vulnerability, is the most powerful and direct way I know of helping people understand that we are all members of the team, that we face challenges—and changes—together. By showing my humanity, I give people reason to trust me. It gives me the credibility and gives my team the confidence we need to adapt and succeed," Eric says.

By opening himself up to his team and providing a workplace in which it is safe to risk trying something new, Eric, as an authentic and humanistic leader, is inviting his staff members to trust him. They find that they can offer their best work, and Eric will encourage their success. If one of them takes a well-thought-out chance and it flops, the important thing will be what was learned in the process. That builds trust and resilience in the team and its members.

In Eric's case, an internal survey suggested it was time for the new approach. The employee engagement survey responses painted a picture of a hostile work environment, one in which challenging the status quo was dangerous to one's career. They reported reluctance to offer personal opinions or to disagree with a superior for fear of retribution.

At first, Eric was stymied; people seldom got fired in his company. Then, he examined his own experience. He had been with the company eight years before being promoted to CEO, just a few years before. When he really thought about it, he remembered feeling the same fear that his employees described.

As he put it, "I began to understand what the survey results were communicating." He decided to open up to his leadership team with honesty and humanism.

"So, during a leadership meeting, I presented the data from the internal surveys. Then, I described my own journey with the company. I told them that, at various times, I had felt very alone and had not contributed alternative viewpoints at meetings. I'd not been particularly candid in meetings, because I had been fearful of being perceived as different or even difficult. I also feared speaking my truth, because I didn't want to be excluded from key activities, such as decision making, etc. Understanding my own behaviors allowed me to really understand the data and to be able to put myself in my employees' shoes.

"Next, I invited my fellow leaders to contribute their own thoughts as to what might be contributing to the perception that we had a culture of fear. Just recounting my own experience really seemed to enable the audience to be quite frank and candid. We had a terrifically honest discussion!"

That particular meeting was a session that LeadQuest had facilitated, so we had the opportunity to witness the impact of Eric's actions firsthand. For the rest of that day, it was as though a firecracker had gone off. People were amazing. They were genuinely enthusiastic, not only opening up to share their own perspectives but encouraging one another's ideas and suggestions. The leadership team has since partnered with staff members to develop a list of items that they identified as contributing to the fear unearthed in the survey, as well as a plan to address them.

In opening up and sharing his own fears, Eric made himself vulnerable—he modeled being a humanistic leader. He also enhanced his credibility as a leader who understands things from his employees' perspective.

Another business leader who understands the concept of being a humanistic manager is Jack Welch, former CEO of General Electric. He describes four types of leaders in his book *Jack: Straight from the Gut.*

A Type IV leader gets desired results through undesired behaviors—i.e., "It's my way or the highway." The unpredictability of this style of leadership, which is often egocentric, ultimately creates an environment of fear. Team members demonstrate compliance behavior—they go along to get along—simply to avoid receiving negative consequences. This type of leader can achieve positive results in the short run, but the results are usually not sustainable over the long haul.

A Type III leader doesn't get results but exhibits desired behavior—i.e., "Kill them with kindness, and everything will be just fine." Another leader on the path to irrelevance, a Type III leader may feel as though s/he is doing all of the right things but actually is pulling the organization and everyone in it down, because results are not being achieved. High performance is about achieving desired results through desired behaviors. Being a nice but incompetent leader hurts morale in an organization as much as a tyrant creates fear in one.

A Type II leader doesn't get desired results and exhibits undesired behavior—i.e., "The whippings will continue until morale (and results) improves." This kind of leader instills first fear and then contempt. The good news is that this type of leader usually doesn't have much credibility within the organization, at any level. S/he typically becomes a "short-timer."

A Type I leader gets desired results though desired behaviors—"We have a job to do; we know what we need to do; and we have the talent to get it done." This leader is authentic—what s/he communicates in the way of performance expectations turns out to be what will produce desired results. This leader is also humanistic—when a team member tries and succeeds, the leader praises the worker and his/her work. When a team member tries but fails, the leader acts as a coach by discussing with that person what was learned and how it can be applied the next time to achieve success. When a team member chooses not to try and fails, a Type I leader quickly takes action to coach the person up to higher performance or out of the organization. The leader is firm but respectful. A Type I leader recognizes that it is not humanistic to let a poor performer continue to fail; it's not fair to that person or to those around him/her.

My experience has shown that Type I leaders draw "want-to" behavior from their team members. Those they lead volunteer their full potential—what they have to give from their hearts as well as from their minds. **This type of leader is able to get "discretionary effort" (i.e., want-to behavior), because s/he builds relationships where trust is at the core**. Family, colleagues, and employees are all happy to give discretionary effort, because their own needs are also being met.

The good news is that a Type I leader is usually the most successful of the four. Being true to himself/herself while being respectful of others, this type of leader—and parent and spouse/partner—models honesty and humility and gains the respect of others in the process. A Type I leader's reward is stronger, richer, and more trusting and committed relationships that produce greater personal satisfaction, success, and happiness.

Principle Two Review: Be authentic and humanistic.

- Being authentic means being honest and true to your beliefs, feelings, and opinions and being willing to share them openly, even in difficult situations.
- Being humanistic means being respectful of others when sharing your beliefs, feelings, and opinions.
- In personal and professional interactions, being authentic and humanistic fosters trust and builds healthy relationships.
- The most effective leader, the Type I humanistic leader, increases desired results by creating a workplace that inspires others to volunteer discretionary effort.

The next chapter will focus on Principle Three: Volunteer discretionary effort constantly. I'll show you how to integrate this concept with the previous principles.

BE AUTHENTIC AND HUMANISTIC: PERSONAL REFLECTION

1. Based on Jack Welch's model, which type of leader would others say you are? What is it about your approach to leadership (i.e., your behavior) that makes this true?

    _____

    _____

    _____

    _____

2. What is the impact of this type of leadership on the relationships you build? On the outcomes you achieve?

    _____

    _____

    _____

    _____

3. Where did you learn to lead this way? Who have you modeled your behavior after? What beliefs have you formed that continue to drive this behavior in you?

    _____

    _____

    _____

    _____

4. Based on the impact they are having on your relationships and results, how well do these beliefs and behaviors serve you today?

    _____

    _____

    _____

    _____

5. How can you be mindful of the impact of your behavior on others, without sacrificing beliefs that are important to you? How can you be humanistic yet still be authentic?

    _____

    _____

    _____

6. What will this look like for you? What impact will an authentic and humanistic approach have on your relationships and results?

_____

_____

_____

_____

Be accountable now!

Chapter Four

Principle Three: Volunteer Discretionary Effort Constantly

. . . .

"The difference between what we do and what we are capable of doing would suffice to solve most of the world's problems."

Mahatma Gandhi

"I want to do it, because I want to do it."

Amelia Earhart

How much do you love your job?

It isn't a trick question. How much joy, how much pride do you take in the work you do? You've heard the proverb: If a job's worth doing, it's worth doing well. Do you believe it?

Beyond the workplace, when it comes to your day-to-day life, how much are you invested in what you do? To find happiness, we have to create it for ourselves in each moment, even in the moments that are given over to getting things done—perhaps especially in those moments.

If the gutters need cleaning, I can dread the nastiness of the job, or I can find some yard gloves and a ladder and take pride in clearing away the leaves and debris so my home will be sound. The gutters serve a purpose that requires that I clean them. No more, no less. I can approach the task with dread or with resolve to do it well. Only one of those choices leads to happiness.

Deciding that a job is worth doing well has a powerful impact, because, as we've discussed, our behavior is driven by what we believe. When I believe that my work has value, I approach it with purpose and pride. Of course, the reverse is also true. If I decide that a particular task is worthless, I'll be miserable doing it and not any happier once it is completed. Taking satisfaction in what I do makes things better, not only for my own well-being but also for those I lead.

We understand that the leader who is in the moment, who is positive, and who inspires others to follow—the Type I leader from the previous chapter—is a person who is authentic and humanistic and brings out the best in people. Aubrey C. Daniels, PhD, defines this concept clearly: "Discretionary effort is defined as that level of effort people could give if they wanted to, but which is beyond what is required."

To understand this term, it's helpful to consider two extreme opposites. One, the personal choice to do only what is absolutely necessary, the *minimum effort* required, is usually inspired by the expected consequences. At work, that might mean *doing only enough to avoid reprimand or even to just keep your job*. At the opposite end of the spectrum is the personal choice to embrace the work that needs to be done—to do work you love and to love the work you do. In this case, the motivation is the process and the anticipated outcomes. This describes what is meant by **discretionary effort—want-to rather than have-to behavior.**

Discretionary effort, then, comes from the personal choice to give one's best, to take pride in the work itself, and to look forward to a job well done. Let's be clear; discretionary effort is not about putting work before all else or sacrificing a well-rounded life. If I choose to give my best in the workplace—to put my best foot forward, as the saying goes—I need to know in my heart that I am equally motivated in every other aspect of my life—at work, at home, and in my personal relationships.

I can achieve this balance when I understand the impact of discretionary effort on my well-being—not just on results and consequences at work. The choice to take a positive approach can lift my spirits. Feeling good about yourself and trusting your instincts help build resilience and create happiness.

Some people seem born with positive attitudes. Take, for example, my childhood neighbor, Kenny.

Kenny started his life with obstacles to overcome. A severe hearing impairment required that he wear two hearing aids (which, in those days, were large and impossible to hide). It also affected his speech, making it sound unnatural and flat and difficult to understand. In the 1950s and '60s, political correctness wasn't even on the horizon. Kids in our neighborhood were merciless in teasing and taunting Kenny. I'm relieved to say I wasn't one of his tormentors. Instead, I found him fascinating.

I got to watch him at work. We lived next door to one another, and at four years my senior, Kenny had the job of mowing his family's lawn. Each week, he cut the grass not only in his own yard but also in the strip between our houses. When he was finished, it was a work of art. I used to love to watch his process. He was a sculptor when it came to trimming the grass, trees, and bushes. This wasn't just work for Kenny; it appeared to be a source of joy.

That was a revelation to me. I had learned the importance of hard work. It was a cornerstone of the household in which I grew up. Hard work was expected, and nothing short of a total commitment to the work was tolerated. In watching Kenny cut his grass or wash his car until it was immaculate and looked new all over again, I saw pride. He approached even mundane work happily and was devoted to doing it well.

I would ask him about this at times, and I can still hear his voice in my head, telling me about the importance of doing things well. He probably didn't realize it at the time, but he was providing a brilliant example.

Kenny became my first mentor, before I'd ever heard the term. He would give me small chores to do, and I was aware that he saw not only what I did but how I did it. Eager to please him, I began to develop a more positive attitude and used him as a model for that attitude. I learned to take pride in my work—not just because it would bring praise, but because it felt good as I did the work itself. When, one day, Kenny handed over the responsibility for our shared yard to me, I felt on top of the world. I had been given a weekly chore to do that was larger than the one my Dad had assigned me—and I loved it!

Learning from Kenny set me on a course to success, even though my father's voice continued to resonate in my head calling me stupid. I had heard from others that I could be something if I tried, and so I did just that.

It would be impossible to overstate the impact of this lesson on my life. In my neighborhood, I became the go-to kid for adults who needed something done. When Kenny's dad needed a delivery made at his florist shop, he called on me. When Miss Irene across the street needed someone to drive her to the store or to the doctor's office, I was the one she called to take her. In my first jobs, I rose to the prime positions quickly—from managing the Shake Shop in town at age sixteen to, in college, driving the tractor for a landscaping company while my peers were relegated to more menial work.

All of this attention and praise served as both positive reinforcement and self-fulfilling prophecy. I enjoyed the reputation I had developed and sought to live up to it. I came to think of myself as a responsible, reliable person, and so I became one. Throughout my career with the phone company—just as in my neighborhood all those years before—I was yet again the go-to guy, the one my superiors called on when they needed something done well.

Even if you grew up in a home environment that didn't provide this type of role model, you can mentor yourself by finding people whose ambition and work you admire. Observe how they manage their lives, their schedules, their workloads, and their personal time. Can you emulate some of their techniques? Can you give yourself a reward when you make progress? Give yourself the positive reinforcement, and enjoy the success you create.

Over the years, I had developed my own positive attitude. I also had developed a reputation for being reliable and dependable. The combination led my supervisors to believe in my ability. More importantly, it taught me a lesson that built my self-confidence.

What I learned was that what differentiated me in this world was the discretionary effort I brought to every task I did, that pride in producing good work gave me a sense of worth. Enough so that, when it came time to leave the security of my phone company job and take a leap of faith to begin my own company, I took it. Even with a family and a mortgage depending on my income, I opted to pursue a career that continues to inspire me and bring me joy.

Looking back on those choices, and upon finding the message in *The Road to Resilience*, I see clearly that this self-confidence not only prepared me well for change but even gave me the courage to take on the biggest personal and professional risk of my life.

I make this point not only to share my happiness but for a more important reason. Very often in my work, I am confronted by someone who is frustrated and angry in his/her job. Let's pick one and call him Jack. Jack tells me he is trapped in a dead-end job. He is well paid but no longer feels challenged. He dreads going to work each day. He is miserable. When I ask Jack what he is doing to improve his situation, he describes his financial responsibilities—a mortgage, tuition for his kids, etc. He feels he cannot afford to leave a job he hates. Those responsibilities are not what created the trap Jack is in. His fear is. The price he pays for this is his happiness.

I see in Jack the expression I used to see on my father's face each day when he returned home from his job at the steel mill. It was clear that he hated his job. He worked for that steel mill for thirty-eight years, and his unhappiness was written all over his face every day. That's why he had such anger about my future, saying, "I'll break both of your arms if you ever work there." If he hated it so much, why did he work there?

Discretionary effort is about choice. People will say, "It's just a job, so what's the big deal?" That flies in the face of taking pride in oneself.

If you're finding that you are miserable in your job, that it is not what you want to do with your life, you can make a change. Even in a difficult economy, you can make a choice (e.g., you can learn a new skill that will enable you to change your circumstances or you can find ways to trim your expenses so that you can afford a pay cut for a while). You are the captain of your own ship. Jack tells me that people depend on him; he needs this job. He tells me that I don't understand.

Yes, I do understand. The beliefs he has about himself, and that his job is just something he does to earn a paycheck, are powerful. They are driving his decision to stay put. Jack has chosen to remain in a position he finds intolerable. He believes that his choices are limited by his responsibilities—and so they are. Putting his financial responsibilities above his own happiness is his choice. Jack's misery, the result of staying in this job, is his choice.

Giving discretionary effort at work can not only improve your own outlook but directly influence your success. It can mean volunteering to speak up. If you're in a meeting, and the discussion has strayed from the agenda, say so respectfully. If you are having trouble following a line of reasoning, speak up and ask for clarification. It can mean going the extra step to deliver a customer's order personally after a snafu in the shipping department. It's asking yourself, "What more can I do right now to make a positive difference?," and acting on the answer. You're accepting accountability for your own participation. We'll talk more about accountability in a future chapter.

One of my clients, the CEO of a hospital, has been able to turn a contentious process into a productive one by giving discretionary effort and asking it of his team. Steve tells me that there has been a long-standing resentment of the regular audits they are required to endure. Consistently, the audit was a struggle, with competing priorities and minimal cooperation.

In seeking to improve the situation, particularly the work relationships, Steve says, "we had to climb out of a pretty deep hole, and I don't know that we're completely out of it yet. But I know we're moving in the right direction."

They began with a meeting to discuss what his team and the audit team had in common and where they differed. "People were a little skeptical. The relationships were really quite poor. It wasn't like we were even working for the same organization. There was a lot of anger. While you intellectually know about needing to work together, it doesn't always happen automatically. It requires intentionality to find the way to do it."

Things improved dramatically once members of both teams opened up. But Steve knew it couldn't stop there. "We have to keep the dialog going. We can't just say, 'we had that meeting back in November.' Before this, communication was only coming at times of mini-crises—not a good time for communicating. We had to agree to put those things on the table." As a result of that first meeting, Steve's team has modified their procedures to improve communications before and after they complete their work.

Steve is working with his team to consistently provide the discretionary effort that will demonstrate their commitment to improving the relationship. "We had been basing our behavior on stuff we made up. If you promise to do something and you do it 80 percent of the time, I start making stuff up about the other 20 percent."

At LeadQuest, discretionary effort takes on a number of different forms. For example, in our dedication to doing the right thing, we reach out to a group of employees who is usually left out of most leadership training classes: the executive assistants. This administrative team is crucial, not only to the success of the leadership team but also in coordinating my work with their company. We work *pro bono* with the executive administrative staff as a matter of practice.

Our willingness to provide this service, to give whatever it takes, is what sets us apart as a company. The effort we make to do the right thing, whether we're compensated or not, gets at the heart of discretionary effort.

On an individual level, what does discretionary effort look like? It is being a role model, serving positively, because that's what is needed. It means holding oneself accountable. It means looking forward to the consequences of actions and taking steps to ensure positive outcomes. People who blame others or the burdens they carry, when they offer minimal effort, are victims of their own beliefs. The problem is in them not outside of them. It is a belief they are creating in their lives that keeps them trapped.

At home, discretionary effort is, first of all, modeling positive behavior for your children. It is encouraging your children to see the joy in the work they do—and recognizing their power to make it joyful—by doing so yourself. It is also helping them to see the connection between their choices and the consequences of those choices. When your son wants something that's outside the family's budget, if the answer is no, it isn't because you have bills to pay, it's because you're saving for his education or for a new home. If your daughter neglects to take out the garbage, it may be educational to let her notice the smell in the garage—and for her to correct it. As a family, you set goals and priorities and sometimes have to make sacrifices to achieve them. Even more valuable, let your children know that you find joy in keeping up your home, in the work you do.

In personal relationships, it's doing what you believe the other person wishes not what you want done. We're familiar with the Golden Rule: "Do unto others as you would have them do unto you." Suppose you took that a step further, striving to treat others the way they wanted to be treated. This approach asks for the intentionality Steve described in his story above. It means opening up to ask those we care about what would make them happy.

If you doubt whether discretionary effort will bring you happiness, try it. You'll find that others notice and appreciate your positive approach. It can even become an example they'll follow.

Principle Three Review: Volunteer discretionary effort constantly.

- Discretionary effort means volunteering effort above and beyond the minimum required; it's the extra "want-to" behavior that increases productivity, etc.
- From sharing an unpopular view in a meeting to going the extra distance for a customer, discretionary effort yields positive benefits in all types of interactions.
- Discretionary effort fosters respect and trust and creates positive feelings and results in all relationships.
- Type I or humanistic leaders create a workplace where people want to volunteer discretionary effort.

The next chapter will focus on Principle Four: Model high performance. Combined with the previous principles, this will help you achieve greater results in all areas of your life.

VOLUNTEER DISCRETIONARY EFFORT CONSTANTLY: PERSONAL REFLECTION

Think about how happy you are right now in your life—in your work and in your personal relationships.

1. Where in your life—at home or at work—do you volunteer discretionary effort? Where don't you? Who or what causes you to give your all in some situations but not in others?

    _____

    _____

    _____

    _____

2. Where you give discretionary effort, what beliefs inspire you to do your best? What impact does this have on your behavior and consequently on your relationships and outcomes—in either environment (work or home)?

    _____

    _____

    _____

    _____

3. If you are unhappy and choosing not to live up to your full potential, what is stopping you from changing your circumstances to become more satisfied with your life and become more effective?

    _____

    _____

    _____

    _____

4. How have you contributed to these circumstances (i.e., what accountability do you have)? What will you do to improve your life? What one or two initial steps will you take *now*?

    _____

    _____

    _____

    _____

Now, suppose you are faced with a fundamental change in your life—you lose your job or, worse, someone you love.

5.   How well prepared are you to face such adversity or change?

_____

_____

_____

_____

6.   What will determine your response? What resources do you have—whether in your relationships or within yourself—that will help you deal with such adversity?

_____

_____

_____

_____

7.   How will your present attitude toward what you do—which influences your behavior and level of discretionary effort—serve you in times of difficult change?

_____

_____

_____

_____

8.   What will you choose to do each day to strengthen your ability to adapt and change?

_____

_____

_____

_____

Be accountable now!

Chapter Five

Principle Four: Model High Performance—Desired Behaviors That Drive Desired Results

· · · · · · · · · · · · · · · · · · · ·

"Example is not the main thing in influencing others. It is the only thing."

Albert Schweitzer

"Keep away from those who try to belittle your ambitions. Small people always do that, but the really great make you believe that you, too, can become great."

Mark Twain

The first three of the Ten Principles of Personal Leadership form the foundation upon which the others build. If we step back for a moment and reflect on those three, we realize that they are all about us, about how we show up in the world, and about the relationships we are able to build when we focus on our own behavior. Healthy behavior and relationships lead to greater resilience, success, and happiness.

Let's review a bit. Principle One—be in the moment—is **choosing to be fully present** for others and oneself. For example, when I'm interacting with someone, I'm able to truly listen to him/her, because I'm giving him/her my undivided attention. This is one of the most powerful ways that I can demonstrate respect for another human being. Principle Two—be authentic and humanistic—is about **being honest while being humble and respectful** of others. I am true to myself yet respectful of the thoughts and feelings of those around me. Principle Three—volunteer discretionary effort constantly—means that I **choose to offer the very best of myself each and every day, in each and every interaction**. In other words, I constantly volunteer effort that goes beyond the minimum that is expected of me. I am demonstrating accountability.

These three principles are all about **what I can control and what I can improve about me**. They are about being present, honest, and respectful and volunteering my very best at all times.

When we add the fourth principle, which is being a role model for high performance—exhibiting desired behaviors that will drive desired results—we introduce the final of the four foundational principles. At LeadQuest, **we define high performance as being equal to desired results plus desired behaviors.** What is worth noting is that when you put these four together, when you choose to live these four principles consistently, your ability to create more trusting relationships grows. In my mind, trusting relationships are at the heart of being able to experience greater resilience, joy, and happiness in this life, and achieving better outcomes and personal success.

High performance, defined as desired results plus desired behaviors, often comes as a surprise to people. Most of my clients have been so focused on achieving desired results (which are, of course, what they're in business to do) that they often don't think about the behavioral aspect to achieving those results. They forget that all business results are achieved through human behavior. It's what people say and do every day that determines whether decision making is skillful and timely, whether work processes run smoothly, and whether strategic or operational plans are executed efficiently and effectively. When the executives with whom I work truly understand the connection between behaviors and results, and that the behaviors they model set the tone for and shape their organizational cultures, then they begin taking the Ten Principles of Personal Leadership to heart.

In my work, I teach two key things:

1. Employees mirror the behaviors of their leaders.
2. Organizational culture (i.e., learned patterns of organizational behavior) eats strategy for lunch.

If I am to be the best leader I can be, I must become a role model for those around me. I must become that Type I leader described in chapter three—the humanistic leader who gets the right results the right way.

Being the sports fan that I am, many of my heroes have been athletes and coaches. One of these coaches, the legendary Woody Hayes of Ohio State University, ruined his reputation in an instant in 1978. As Ohio State was playing Clemson for the Gator Bowl trophy, Coach Hayes chose to punch a Clemson football player. The player had just made a key interception and had been pushed out of bounds at Woody Hayes's feet on the Ohio State sideline. I can remember watching that game and Coach Hayes's behavior, and I was shocked. A man whom so many people looked up to, one of the most successful coaches in NCAA football history, exhibited behavior that was not only unsportsmanlike but under other circumstances might have been viewed as criminal. That day, I could not help but wonder what kind of example Coach Hayes had just set for the student body of Ohio State and for the millions of people watching the game.

If we fast-forward to the current day, there are more and more stories hitting the airwaves about parents who end up fighting with one another or exhibiting other shameful behavior at youth league sporting events. The message that I believe they are communicating is that winning is the only thing. It doesn't matter how you win. It's as though sportsmanship—how you conduct yourself on the playing field and off—seems to have gotten lost. More and more professional athletes, whom the kids of America look up to, are making poor behavioral choices and hence becoming poor role models for generations of young people.

As on the sports field, when we accept a low standard of interpersonal behavior in the workplace—one that puts winning and the bottom line ahead of our personal values and the respectful treatment of coworkers—we often set up conflict within ourselves and with those with whom we work. **Organizational leaders who model (and thereby encourage) undesired behavior, including unhealthy competition between coworkers, communicate the message that you must ignore your own values (and probably, those professed by the company) in order to be successful.** Not only is this bad leadership, but it is bad business, because it ends up hurting employee morale and the bottom line. What the leaders I coach and support have come to appreciate is that being a successful leader doesn't mean you have to give up being a good person. They are accountable for both, and the Ten Principles teach us how to be both.

In my own life, the conflict between what was expected of me at work— to be a politically savvy person who did what he had to do to win—and the behavior required of me to be a loving husband and father at home became the first step to my creating LeadQuest and taking up the line of work I find so fulfilling today.

In my last position at the phone company, that conflict became a deal breaker. A new executive was brought in from outside the company to be president of my business unit. I reported directly to him. This guy was highly egocentric; as I recall, I imagined that he viewed himself as God's gift to us. Shortly after his arrival, he began making sexist comments and flirting openly with women in the office. I found that offensive and disrespectful; I often wondered what his wife would have thought about his behavior. For a while, though, I believed I had no choice but to "go along to get along" with him. Even today, I can clearly remember the moment when I'd had enough—the moment when a woman stepped off the elevator, and he made a comment to me, appraising her physique. That time I didn't smile at him and nod in agreement. Instead, I allowed my expression to be true to my values. I reflected my own disgust rather than going along.

Ultimately, I chose to take a demotion rather than continue working with him. In the process, I told him that our values were incompatible. I remember that he was shocked that I would take a demotion (his punishment for me "wanting out") and give up a promising career rather than continue working for him. Two months later, I quit the company where I had worked for fifteen years, and I formed LeadQuest. I know he was not unique and that there are many more people (like me) struggling to earn a living and succeed in the workplace without having to sacrifice their values. There are leaders whose values and resulting behaviors not only offend those who report to them but contradict the values espoused by the companies they lead.

Before I decided to leave, I went to that man's boss, who had been my mentor and a personal hero, and I asked his advice. He agreed that the man's behavior was deplorable, but he advised me to look the other way. Although he and I continue to be friends, I'll never believe that was good advice.

In those places where the profits and bottom-line results are the exclusive priority, fear-based cultures often are created. The employees who remain in those organizations are compliant and fearful and not committed to doing their very best work. Results are suboptimized. People don't volunteer discretionary effort. In my seminars, when I ask audience members what percentage of their employees give discretionary effort, the answer I get back from leaders (representing a myriad of industries) is typically less than 40 percent. When I ask why that is the case, the answer is usually "unmotivated" or "lazy" employees. Upon hearing that, I immediately challenge those leaders to look in the mirror to see how they contribute to the dynamic.

What I and the leaders with whom I work have learned is that **leadership that is true to the values of the company**—that rewards authentic and respectful behavior as much as it does technical skill—**produces better results**. When those doing the work feel respected, rather than in conflict, they are inspired to respect themselves and others. In the end, they want to volunteer their best; they are accountable and resilient in the face of change and adversity.

What is most rewarding to me in my work with leaders is that, more and more, undesired behavior is no longer being tolerated. That goes well beyond the workplace regulations that now prohibit discrimination based on gender, age, religion, or ethnicity. I see greater awareness of the connection between interpersonal behaviors and results. The leaders I support are now choosing to "coach people up or out" of the company, based on the interpersonal behaviors those people exhibit.

I define organizational culture as being learned patterns of behavior. Often, undesired patterns of behavior are positively reinforced, because, as Dr. Aubrey C. Daniels would say, "doing nothing is doing something." **Choosing to not address undesired behavior (to do nothing) is actually a choice, conscious or not, to reinforce it.** If we want more fulfilling outcomes, in our personal life or at work, we must return to the original Golden Rule: Treat others as you wish they would treat you. Better yet, treat others the way they want to be treated.

Carol is one of the executives with whom I work who has seen the power of Principle Four—modeling high performance—in shaping and improving her personal leadership and the effectiveness of her team. She says, "We used to have a real culture of distrust here. Work was not getting done, and my team spent a lot of time blaming others. It wasn't until I started working on the Ten Principles that I saw that, as a leader, I was responsible for that behavior.

"I used to multitask so much I never really got anything done. I had the habit of taking work into a meeting, thinking I'd save time on the other end. I didn't focus directly on the issue at hand. I was not being as effective as I could be, and I was certainly modeling behavior that was not collaborative or productive.

"Now that I'm committed to living the Ten Principles, people have noticed the changes in me. One thing they've noticed is that I come into meetings without other work to do, and I'm focused on the issues on the agenda. I'm a far better contributor and role model.

"And I'm seeing that same focus in my team. We aren't perfect, but there is much less rework, less redoing of jobs we need to get done efficiently.

"This principle has been powerful for me in terms of realizing what my role should be as a leader. I'm recognizing that I am accountable for shaping the right culture. What was happening before was a lot of blaming and triangulation. *My 'aha' moment came when I realized that it starts with me.* My team knows that I'm not perfect, but I'm working hard to be in the moment and to be authentic and humanistic. Their behavior is better now too."

In recognizing and embracing her own accountability, Carol has inspired the same ownership in her team.

In my work, I ask executives to consider both technical and interpersonal behaviors—both are needed to produce high-performance results. I'll ask which of the two is more challenging in the workplace. The answer I get back, without fail, is interpersonal behaviors. We tend to believe that we can teach the technical but not the interpersonal. I disagree. I think *we teach interpersonal behaviors in all of our interactions through the modeling we do for others.* When we embrace the opportunities to model and teach interpersonal behaviors, we realize the importance of the example we set. As Mahatma Gandhi famously challenged, "Be the change you want to see in the world."

Companies often promote people because of their technical skills. We take skilled technicians and promote them into leadership positions, because they get great results as individual contributors. This is often unfair to them as well as to the people who report to them. Why? Because they don't possess the managerial and interpersonal skills needed to be successful. When you're hiring and promoting, it is as critical to focus on the interpersonal behaviors as it is to pay attention to the technical. **Great leaders don't have to be subject-matter experts.** They can surround themselves with experts. **They have to understand their responsibilities as leaders.** A great leader has to master interpersonal skills and be able to build strong relationships, teams, and organizations.

Outside of the workplace, I believe the most profound leadership role is the one undertaken by parents. As parents, it is more important than ever that we set the right example for our children. We have to treat them with respect—using the Ten Principles—by being in the moment for them, by being authentic and humanistic with them, and by volunteering discretionary effort when spending time with them. It's when these principles come together and work for us in harmony that we model for our children the pathway to success and happiness. They learn best when they see us holding ourselves accountable and being resilient in the face of challenge.

If they are to create a better world, where unity and trusting relationships help them achieve success by working with others rather than stepping on or over others, we have to show them the way.

If our goal for our children (or our employees) is for them to succeed in business, we have to show them that we are the same people at work, living the same values, speaking the same truths, as we are at home. If our goal for our children is to be well liked, they need to see us being in the moment and being authentic and humanistic—i.e., they need to see us building trusting relationships.

When they see us being true to our values and finding happiness in that, they can more easily see the path to their own happiness.

Principle Four Review: Model high performance—desired behaviors that drive desired results.

- High performance is defined as desired results plus desired behaviors, because human behavior produces results.
- Employees mirror the behavior of their leaders.
- Organizational leaders who model and reinforce undesired behavior communicate the message that you must ignore your own values in order to be successful there.
- Leadership that is true to the values of the company, that rewards authentic and humanistic behavior as much as it does technical skill, produces better results.

The next chapter will focus on Principle Five: Respect and leverage separate realities. Combined with authentic and humanistic leadership, this principle will highlight the role that human differences (i.e., diversity) play in producing stronger relationships *and* results.

Model High Performance—Desired Behaviors That Drive Desired Results: Personal Reflection

Think about how you behaved today at work and how you acted when you arrived at home.

1. How were you the same in those two environments? How were you different?

    _____
    _____
    _____
    _____

2. How well do you live your values at work? What behaviors are you modeling for those around you? Would you be able to tell others "Do as I do" rather than "Do as I say"?

    _____
    _____
    _____
    _____

3. What causes you to behave this way? What kind of thinking drives this behavior?

    _____
    _____
    _____
    _____

4. Are there certain situations that cause you to behave contrary to your values? Certain people? If so, how does that conflict make you feel about yourself? What are the results you are getting?

    _____
    _____
    _____
    _____

5. How about at home—what are you modeling for those closest to you? As a result, what behavior do you see in them? How satisfied are you with this?

_____

_____

_____

_____

6. How do you want to be remembered by your colleagues and family?

_____

_____

_____

_____

7. Based on what you are currently modeling, how will you be remembered?

_____

_____

_____

_____

8. What will you do, right now, to model high performance at work and at home?

_____

_____

_____

_____

Be accountable now!

Chapter Six

Principle Five: Respect and Leverage Separate Realities

· · · · · · · · · · · · · · · · · · · ·

"Because every human being lives a separate reality, it's impossible for two human beings, from the same culture or not, to see things precisely alike."

Richard Carlson

"Two heads are better than one."

Unknown

Each one of us has a unique perspective. From the time we were born, we've received messages and consequences from all the experiences we have had that have shaped the way we see the world and the people and events in it. This creates for each of us a unique set of "filters," through which we interpret what happens around us. In other words, **each of us is living a separate reality.** These separate realities give rise to a diversity of perceptions, beliefs, and behaviors.

What we tend to forget is that each one of us also has blind spots. My reality is limited by my personal experiences, by my filters. Those filters create my blind spots. I perceive the world according to my reality, which is, by definition, different from the way you perceive it. I am blind to some things, including your individual perception and personal viewpoint.

When I stop and think about the vastness of what I don't know or understand, it makes sense to approach life and people from a place of humility. Approaching life from a place of humility ties in with Principle Two—being authentic and humanistic. Egocentricity, thinking and acting as if I know everything, as if I possess all the answers, no longer makes sense. The fact that I don't have all the answers should cause me to recognize that I have blind spots that can inhibit building relationships and achieving greater success. If I hope to succeed and be happy, I should seek to learn from the perceptions and experiences of others and then leverage them for the greater good.

Principle Five—respecting and leveraging separate realities—begins with that self-awareness, with respecting others and their individual realities. **I understand that someone can see something differently than I do and that we can both be right.** This is an uncomfortable concept for many people who have reached leadership positions. It feels like a lack of confidence. Seen differently and accountably, it requires great confidence and courage to accept that my perception might not be entirely accurate or complete.

Suppose you and I witness an argument. We can reach completely different conclusions about which person was the aggressor. If we look more closely at our own perceptions, we might find that the person whose side I took is someone I admired or that you objected to his/her approach, because s/he used language that you found objectionable. Each of us had a filter that determined how we experienced the argument and led to our individual conclusions (and, incidentally, neither of us usually has enough information to truly understand the circumstances of the argument itself, let alone the realities of the participants). Yet, we each reached separate conclusions, certain that we were correct. The argument had a reality that was determined for each of us by our own set of filters.

Now apply the same logic to problem solving. Suppose you and I have been charged with creating a plan to reduce costs. If we both approach the challenge, believing that our own reality is accurate and above question, we come to the table with less to offer. We have limited our solutions before we've even begun to address the problem together.

That happens because we each come with a set of beliefs that we are ready to protect. Perhaps I have decided that my area of the company is too vital to be trimmed, or you have decided that I have a hidden agenda. Our perceptions become barriers to reaching the best solution and being fully accountable to our boss and our organization.

Suppose, on the other hand, we begin by believing that we both have the best of intentions. We both remain aware of our own limited perspectives and welcome the opportunity to learn from one another. I choose to accept that even my work area could be run more efficiently, and you choose to accept that we have a common goal to do what's best for the company. We've opened up the scope of possible solutions.

By acknowledging separate realities, the only thing either of us has relinquished is our preconceived notions, and what we have gained are resources for addressing the challenge of cutting costs. It's one thing to accept that others see things differently than I do. The real power of this principle becomes available to me when I choose to leverage these separate realities.

What erodes relationships, teamwork, and creativity is when we react to someone else's reality in a negative way and assume that his/her intention is self-serving or harmful. This typically occurs when we are not in the moment. *If I am not truly present, I am especially vulnerable to blind spots.* I fall back on the autopilot thoughts and reactions that we discussed in chapter one. If I am convinced that my own perception is accurate and find that it doesn't match yours, I will conclude that I'm right and you're wrong. I will stop listening.

As closely as I strive to live these Ten Principles, I still sometimes find myself clutching to my reality in a way that undermines my encounters with others and has the potential to damage my relationships. When I pause and reflect on what I have contributed to this dynamic, I usually realize that I have not been in the moment; I have not been fully present, engaged, and open.

This even happens when I am working with groups of clients on the principles themselves. Occasionally, a participant will challenge what I have to say. If I listen openly, seeking to understand his/her reality, I can then respond in a way that is humanistic, that acknowledges the contribution without taking the group off track. If I am distracted—and sometimes it is the person's tone or my own negative thoughts that distract me—I lose focus and stop listening, turning instead to defending my own position, which is my autopilot response.

For me, this can be a matter of confidence. When I am not open to his/her perspective, it is often a response to my own deep-seated insecurities. I'm right back in my parent's house, hearing my father tell me I'm not good enough or my mother worry about what others will think. I have coached enough clients to realize that this is a struggle for many of us. None of us is at our best when we allow ourselves to be driven by this kind of fear. **Insecurity often leads to egocentricity.**

The beauty of the Ten Principles, for me and for my clients, is that they provide a framework for being purposeful about how we show up in the world. The more I strive to be in the moment, the more I recognize when I am not listening openly and actively, the more disciplined and respectful I become. I am better prepared to extinguish my internal demons. It is, indeed, a matter of progress and not one of perfection. Being in the moment is the door opener to recognizing and leveraging the perspectives of others.

One of the executives I've worked with, Brian, has learned not only to recognize but also to leverage individual realities in an especially powerful way.

"There is one direct report of mine that used to get on my nerves all the time. In a lot of our encounters, my perception was that he was whining. We'd get into a discussion, and it seemed as though everything he said was about 'me, me, me' [i.e., him]. It sounded to me like a lot of whining that had nothing to do with solving the problem.

"When I started working with Principle Five, I learned to control my emotions and leverage our interactions better by looking past my perception of his whining to hear the useful things he had to say. I listened more closely and focused on his positive contributions. Gradually, I realized that when I had focused on him as a whiner, I had only been seeing about 2 percent of this guy's potential, because I hadn't been listening to all he had to offer.

"Once I was open to that, I worked on engaging him in finding solutions for things. In the past, I had been looking for the flaw, so it was all I saw. Now, not only do I hear more of what he has to contribute, but he is contributing more and being less negative."

As I listened to Brian's story—and as I repeat it here—it occurs to me that, by being willing to see this man as something other than a whiner, Brian encouraged him to whine less. By respecting the man's separate reality, by being open to the possibility that there was more to him than whining, Brian gave himself leverage to draw more from him and to improve his contributions to the challenges at hand.

When we accept accountability for the blind spots in our own perceptions of reality, we gain perspective. If you've ever been a parent, you've had the opportunity to learn this lesson from your kids. The child who complains, "You never let me do anything I want" is certainly exaggerating but probably isn't entirely wrong. There might be room to ease up on the controls and give your child a chance to test his/her own wings (in an appropriately safe setting). If she's eight, she might be ready to choose her own clothes. If he's sixteen and responsible, he might be ready for a driver's license.

As clear as this is to me now, it isn't at all how we have historically prepared our leaders. In society, and especially in business, we value confidence. Based on my experience in the business world, I've observed that people who are promoted into leadership positions are people who are clear-minded and reach firm decisions quickly. **We encourage a certainty that doesn't require those leaders to leverage or even respect separate realities.**

So when might confidence become arrogance? When I tell myself I have all the answers, when I fail to value and listen to the separate realities of those around me, when, consequently, I leave members of my team feeling disenfranchised and disrespected, I become an arrogant—and a much less effective—leader. At the logical end of this path is a leader who is surrounded by sycophants and making decisions that are limited by his/her personal reality.

It isn't hard to make this leap, even if you don't intend to become a tyrant. Sometimes, the perception we fail to see is the one that others have of us. People in leadership positions are especially vulnerable to this blind spot. One of my clients, Greta, discovered this some time after she'd become a senior executive.

"There is this trap that I didn't see before. It comes up when I'm speaking to my team. I see them nod, and they act like they're in agreement. I think they understand and truly agree with what I'm saying.

"I forget that some people think they need to look like they are in agreement with me. I don't necessarily want that. It's a funny thing that happens when you get into a top position—people are a lot more agreeable. It's not that they understand or that we've had enough good dialogue about what we're going to do. I've learned that they nod because they think that's what they ought to do. In other words, they've become conditioned to do that when working with authority figures.

"Since I've been working on the Ten Principles, I've worked really hard to make sure people on my staff understand that they can speak up if they don't agree with me. I feel like I used to be open to that, but when I took this role, it did change, and I was unaware of that change. It became harder to reach true consensus.

"Now I watch their faces closely and ask, 'Do you disagree?' 'Were you thinking of something else?' I encourage them to speak up so that we all understand one another well and are clear on what we're agreeing to. I think the best solutions come from that."

Greta has not only grasped the value of separate realities, she considers it her responsibility to leverage them. It has made her a stronger leader. By seeking to understand before acting, **she achieves buy-in and ownership from her team. The team is stronger, more prepared to undertake new challenges.**

Each of us wants to feel like we have made a contribution. In the workplace, we have learned lessons that we have found valuable to getting the job done. We want our expertise to be acknowledged and put to use. We understand and can inform best practices. For leaders who grasp and leverage this, the benefits are manifold. First, these leaders must be prepared to respect the separate realities of their employees.

The number one driver of employee satisfaction is the quality of the relationship that exists between a subordinate and his/her boss. A common complaint I hear is that people do not feel that their opinions are valued. The fact that their bosses don't solicit their input or actively listen to them when they do has two powerful results: 1) the boss misses the opportunity to learn from and leverage their experiences, and 2) morale sinks. The impact on business results is always negative, contrary to the results the boss wants.

When, as a leader, you recognize that you have blind spots and view this as an opportunity rather than as a weakness, you gain information and creativity that maximizes the team's productivity and enhances the quality of your own leadership.

Accepting help and support from those you care about and who will listen to you **strengthens resilience and inspires discretionary effort.**

This isn't the way most of us were conditioned to lead. My generation was taught that a leader must be prepared with all of the answers. Admitting that there was something I didn't know and accepting that I might be wrong was considered a fatal flaw, a sign of weakness. Many of us learned that it was better to fake expertise than admit we had something to learn. It's a conditioning we have to break in order to lead high-performing teams. This paradigm shift—and the Ten Principles that guide us through it—becomes even more important as a new generation that expects to be heard enters and advances in the work force.

When I am willing to live the foundational principles, I can choose to pause and listen actively to understand your viewpoint(s). I'll be fully present. I'll be honest with myself and humble enough to recognize my blind spots. I'll be respectful and volunteer the openness I know will lead us both to a better understanding of one another. In doing these things, I'll show myself and you that I welcome you and your ideas.

Respecting separate realities leads you to move from tolerance to acceptance to leveraging the ideas of others. **High-performing teams are those that build on, rather than diminish or restrain, their separate realities.**

This principle is about more than just respecting separate realities, after all. Leveraging separate realities leads to stronger relationships, to better decision making, to joint accountability, to greater resilience, and to better results. The reason we reach these outcomes is that we sincerely choose to pursue a path of respectful inquiry. We are willing to engage in robust discussions and respectful debates. We are willing to leverage the ideas in the room to achieve a shared goal, decision, or resolution.

When we talk and share and explore ideas that originated from our individual realities, we open the door to creativity and innovation. We are greater than the sum of our parts.

Another outcome of leveraging our separate realities is that we reach true consensus and alignment toward shared goals. Individually, we each implement the steps to reach those goals with the kind of commitment and discretionary effort that drives success.

Principle Five Review: Respect and leverage separate realities.

- Each of us is living a separate reality. These separate realities give rise to a diversity of beliefs, perceptions, and behaviors.
- Because you are living a separate reality, you have your own unique blind spots.
- By acknowledging separate realities, you understand that someone can see something differently than you do and that you can both be right.
- Accepting help and support from those you respect strengthens resilience and inspires discretionary effort.
- Respecting separate realities enables you to move from tolerance to acceptance to leveraging the ideas of others. High-performing teams are those that build on, rather than diminish or restrain, their separate realities.

The next chapter will focus on Principle Six: Be curious vs. judgmental. This principle goes hand in hand with Principle Five and will enable you to respect and leverage separate realities.

RESPECT AND LEVERAGE SEPARATE REALITIES: PERSONAL REFLECTION

Reflect on today's interactions and how clearly you saw what was going on around you at work and at home.

1. How many separate realities did you come into contact with at work today?

    _____
    _____
    _____
    _____

2. How did you respond? To what extent do you really explore the separate realities of your peers, subordinates, or boss?

    _____
    _____
    _____
    _____

3. How does your behavior impact your ability to leverage separate realities to achieve higher performance?

    _____
    _____
    _____
    _____

4. Why is it critical to be in the moment in order to respect separate realities?

    _____
    _____
    _____
    _____

5. What separate realities do you encounter at home?

    _____
    _____
    _____
    _____

6. At home, is there anyone whose separate reality you do not need to respect and leverage? Why (or why not)?

_____

_____

_____

_____

7. What can you do each day to more intentionally respect and leverage the separate realities of others at work and at home?

_____

_____

_____

_____

Be accountable now!

Chapter Seven

Principle Six: Be Curious vs. Judgmental

. . . .

"Seek first to understand then to be understood."

Stephen Covey

"We are all inclined to judge ourselves by our ideals; others, by their acts."

Harold Nicolson

One of the most powerful ways we can respect separate realities is to come from curiosity when we encounter someone whose reality differs from our own. **Curiosity means that I am willing to ask questions and listen actively to fully understand where someone is coming from—i.e., I seek to understand his/her reality.** In order to do this skillfully, I must be in the moment, be authentic and humanistic, and volunteer discretionary effort.

The distractions seem endless—and often negative. We are bombarded with negative messages, especially in this multimedia age of 24/7 "infotainment." Over and over, we are told that one thing is considered better than another, usually for superficial reasons. We are told that thin is better than fat, tall is better than short, winning is better than playing well, being a white-collar worker is better than being a blue-collar worker, and so on and so on. We live in a judgmental world; this is so much the case that our inner voice becomes highly critical. It is no surprise that most of us have learned to assess things and even people at face value—and often negatively.

This isn't something innate in humans. This is something we learn as we grow and are educated in society. One of my core beliefs is that we are born innocent and curious. Our true nature at birth is to assume the best in others. The fact that we have learned to judge one another means that we can learn not to judge. We can break harmful patterns and learn a better way.

How quickly do you form a first impression? When I ask others that question, the answers I usually get are "instantaneously" or "within a minute or two." The answers come promptly and confidently. When I probe and ask what that impression is based on, they tell me it's a matter of the person's looks or clothes or speech or mannerisms. Based on my experience, if those standards do not match my own, I, typically on autopilot, judge the person negatively. I say that s/he made a bad first impression, and I move on. Whether I realize it or not, I probably also convey the message that s/he is not worthy of my attention.

So what is wrong with this picture? How can we possibly know or really, truly understand others within the first few minutes of meeting them? The answer is: we can't.

Unfortunately, many of us view our own reality, which includes our own standards, as being the absolute or best reality. Another name for this is egocentricity. When I operate with the belief that I am right, I separate myself from others and feel free to accept or dismiss them out of hand. I place myself above them, and in most cases, they know it.

Remember, my relationship with you can only be as good as the conversation I have about you in my mind. In other words, my thinking and beliefs about you drive my behaviors toward you.

There is an important distinction we need to make here between making clear judgments and being judgmental. *Merriam Webster's Collegiate Dictionary, Eleventh Edition* **defines judgment as "the process of forming an opinion." It defines judgmental as "characterized by a tendency to judge harshly."**

Every day we are required to make choices, decisions, and judgments. Should I wear this outfit? Is this the best route to take? Whom should I appoint? Who is best prepared to lead this project? On their own, these decisions or judgments are neutral. It's how we make them—e.g., our willingness to criticize others—that determines whether we are coming from curiosity or being judgmental. If I am curious, I am open to seeing the best in others and in their ideas.

When I hear that someone has been promoted and I tell coworkers it was a stupid decision, I'm being judgmental. If, on the other hand, I accept that I don't have all the answers and begin to ask myself what I'm not seeing in the person who was promoted, my curiosity can be helpful. My own egocentric approach, my judgment of others, led me to a negative conclusion. Curiosity has the potential to lead to a positive one.

In my neighborhood, there was one guy, in particular, whom was admired by my father. Even though I hadn't met Binky (his nickname), I knew all about him. When I was very young, my father would talk with Binky and later tell me about him, about what a great guy he was. Binky was a tall, handsome, young man. He was a scholar-athlete in high school and college. He graduated from Harvard and from there got a high-paying job on Wall Street.

When I was beginning my own career at the phone company, I used to visit my parents, who were still living in our old neighborhood. Once, I stopped by the local convenience store and looked up when I heard the cashier tell his friends, "Here comes that moron again for his cigarettes." He was barely back out the door when the group began joking about the bone-thin, disheveled man. The same straggly guy passed by our house about an hour later, and my father looked at him and shook his head, saying, "What a shame." The boy who had held such promise and this man who had been so easily dismissed at the store were one and the same—Binky! I was devastated. My mother explained that, earlier that year, Binky, who was in his mid-thirties at the time, had returned home a wreck after having a nervous breakdown.

It broke my heart to think that this once-promising paragon had been judged so harshly. They didn't know him! They pronounced him a moron, knowing nothing about him. Naturally, they treated him like one too. He deserved better.

Of course, it's easy to recognize when others are being judgmental. Very often, we jump to conclusions about the way others behave. We forget that people do things for reasons that are clear to them. With the possible exception of cartoon characters, no one intentionally sets out to create trouble or upset others; however, intention does not always equal impact. When we are curious rather than judgmental, we remember that we are all just trying to do our best.

Otherwise, we act like Gary.

Gary headed to an executive retreat one Monday morning in his brand new car. Arriving early, he parked carefully to limit the chances that anyone would damage it. He painstakingly backed his car into a corner spot, well clear of the line dividing his parking space from the adjacent one. He reasoned that that would put him far out of reach of the driver's door of any car that parked next to his.

At the lunch break, Gary looked out the window to check on his prized possession only to find someone had not only parked in the space next to his, but had backed in and parked right on top of the dividing line. The offending car couldn't possibly be closer to his new one and still be in its own space. Gary was outraged. How could anyone have been so stupid?

Strong personality that he was, Gary walked out to the lot and looked at the car of his new enemy. There were enough personal details (a bumper sticker, a parking pass, etc.) to establish the owner's identity. Gary challenged the offender at the next break.

"What the hell were you thinking?" he asked.

It should be pointed out that in telling this story months later, Gary readily acknowledged that, while asking someone to explain his actions might actually seem like curiosity, it was clear in this case that he had judged the other driver. The day had offered plenty of time for conversations in his mind about this other driver, and in each one, he had judged the offender a thoughtless scoundrel who lacked respect for other people's property.

Luckily, the other driver understood Gary's perspective and had an ego to match his. Once Gary cooled down, the driver explained that he had purposefully parked where he had, certain that, of all the drivers with cars on the lot, he and Gary were likely to be the most careful. He would be cautious not only with his own car but with Gary's as well. In his mind, both cars were as safe as could be.

Because he ultimately took the time to listen, Gary emerged from what began as a heated exchange feeling better about his colleague—if a little poorly about himself. In accosting his fellow driver and coworker, had he asked a question? Yes. Was that question judgmental? Certainly. Had he been truly curious, however, Gary would have asked a very different question. Had he paused to reconsider the conversation he was having about the other driver in his head, he might have taken a different approach or even decided that, as no harm had come to his new car, the perceived offense was not an actual one and not worth pursuing.

People's behavior makes sense to them. Rather than leap to the judgment that someone is crazy (or inconsiderate or foolish), it is far healthier and more productive to wonder what it is that made sense to him/her. We are calmer, and it is easier to remain in the moment when we assume the best of others.

When I judge another person harshly, I cheat both of us out of potential happiness. Relationships are a key contributor to our happiness. If you live your life judgmentally, no one will ever meet your standards, and you will never have meaningful relationships. You will continually place yourself either above or below others, missing out on what you have in common. If, on the other hand, you remain open to seeing the best in others, to believing that they, like you, are trying to live good lives, your curiosity will open doors to stronger relationships.

Often times, the person you continually judge harshly is yourself. You have high standards—you consider yourself a perfectionist—and you almost always conclude that you fail to meet them. Being judgmental toward yourself closes the door to self-awareness and growth and separates you from others. It prevents you from being in the moment. **If you are not humanistic with yourself, you cannot be truly humanistic with others.** You will not find happiness. Learning this powerful lesson in my own life has freed me from the bondage of insecurity and unhappiness.

Being judgmental (not humanistic) toward others makes us closed to their separate realities. In conversation, if what's being said doesn't fit our reality, we tend to go out of the moment and to judge. We tend to oversimplify and dismiss without exploring, much less hearing, the other person's point of view. However, I can choose to suspend my judgment until I've heard and can understand the other person's perspective. Once that happens, even if we disagree, we have treated one another with respect. Harsh judgment tears that respect down, erodes trust, and leaves no one whole.

One CEO we work with, Karen, offers an example of the transformative power of choosing curiosity over judgment. Like Gary, she acknowledges that she isn't a perfect model for the Ten Principles she is striving to live by, but she is making progress.

"I was in the process of filling a leadership position and had someone I wanted to hire. I had pretty much jumped to the conclusion that this was the right candidate for the job. In retrospect, I can say that, in an effort to make it *appear* to be a fair and balanced process, I solicited some feedback along the way. I have to say, though, I was determined to hire my candidate.

"Even though I had publicly sought some feedback, one particular board member was very angry about my choice. I decided to set up a follow-up meeting with him.

"[In the meantime,] the candidate I chose declined the position. He indicated that there was much too much angst in the organization about my choice for him to be successful."

When the time came to meet with the board member, Karen realized that she could stand her ground and staunchly defend her decision or she could be curious and listen actively to his concerns.

"There was a time when I would have gone into the conversation with this board member ready with all of the reasons why I had completed the process that I had; I can be very convincing. This time I decided not to do that. I just sat down with him and said 'I need to understand where you're coming from. Help me understand.'

"He told me I hadn't gotten enough appropriate input; I hadn't gotten the right people involved. I had jumped to a conclusion. After listening to him, I said, 'You know what? You're right. That is what happened. Where do we go from here? How do we move this process forward?'

"We ended up with a different process—a much better process—and different candidates. We hired a much better candidate, who has become thoroughly engaged. I also improved my relationship with a board member who cared enough about our company to speak up and challenge me.

"We ended up with a much better outcome."

When we choose humility and choose to involve others appropriately in decision making, welcoming their ideas and suspending judgment in favor of doing what is best for the organization, our decisions are enriched. We have drawn from an enhanced pool of experience and ideas. The participants are more likely to approach their next challenges with the same openness and willingly take the accountability to share their ideas and concerns.

When we choose to be judgmental, people feel devalued and as though their ideas aren't worth anything, and often they don't say anything. They become frustrated and defensive. This inhibits discretionary effort and high performance.

When we are not humanistic or respectful of separate realities, our decisions and choices can become judgmental. How I make those decisions when they involve other people and how I communicate those choices to those who will have to live with them determines whether I am behaving in a way that is humanistic and respectful or judgmental.

When I approach my decisions with curiosity, I solicit and actively listen to the opinions of others who will be affected by the outcome. When I respect and leverage their separate realities, the entire process is enriched. Shortcutting the process to make it easier on me can lead to less effective decision making. There are times when we need to accept the responsibility of leadership and make judgments in the moment. Even those decisions are enriched if, as a leader, I think of myself and my decisions in terms of how they will impact those around me. If I am in the moment, I can make sound decisions quickly without being on autopilot.

In any group, whether I am the leader or a member of the team, when I remember that I can only change myself, the responsibility for being open and curious rather than judgmental is mine. I can contribute to better decision making with a personal commitment to this principle.

This will not only yield stronger decision making by the team but open the way to better relationships in my own life. It is an important key to achieving happiness.

Principle Six Review: Be curious vs. judgmental.

- Curiosity is being willing and eager to ask questions and listen actively to fully understand where others are coming from—i.e., seek to understand their realities.
- Judgment is defined as "the process of forming an opinion." Being judgmental is defined as "characterized by a tendency to judge harshly."
- First impressions of others are often inappropriately judgmental.
- It's easier to recognize when others are being judgmental than when we are being judgmental.
- People's behaviors make sense to them (based on their realities).
- When we choose humility and choose to involve others in decision making—welcoming their ideas and suspending judgment in favor of doing what is best for the organization—trust and discretionary effort increase, and our decisions are enriched.

Based on our work with the previous principles, chapter eight focuses on an important concept: Look in the mirror first—be accountable. This ties in directly with all the other principles and is key to taking ownership and control of your life.

BE CURIOUS VS. JUDGMENTAL: PERSONAL REFLECTION

1. Are there people you encounter at work with whom you tend to be judgmental? What conversations are you having about them in your mind?

    _____

    _____

    _____

    _____

2. How does that impact your relationships and results? What will you do to repair those relationships so you can achieve better outcomes?

    _____

    _____

    _____

    _____

3. Are there certain situations you encounter at work in which you tend to be judgmental? How does that impact your results? Remember, high performance is modeling desired behaviors that will drive desired results.

    _____

    _____

    _____

    _____

4. How quickly do you become judgmental at home? How does that impact your relationships and your happiness? What do you need to do (i.e., which principles do you need to apply) to improve your ability to remain curious and open-minded at home?

    _____

    _____

    _____

    _____

5. What impact will being curious vs. judgmental have on your life? On your happiness?

_____

_____

_____

_____

Be accountable now!

Chapter Eight

Principle Seven: Look in the Mirror First—Be Accountable

• •

"Ask not what your country can do for you. Ask what you can do for your country."

John F. Kennedy

"The fault, dear Brutus, is not in our stars, but in ourselves."

William Shakespeare

There is only one person I can control and change; that person is me. **I am in control of the choices I make.** For example, do I complain about my job, or do I bring my very best to improving it? Do I try to change my spouse, or do I celebrate and learn from his/her different perspective? Do I act as though I am held hostage by my family responsibilities, or do I accept ownership of my situation and seek to improve it? In marriage, at work, in life—each of us seems to need to be reminded that we are the captains of our own ships.

Given this, the first important question to ask is, "How have I contributed to each of these situations?" The second is, "What more will I do to improve or change them?"

If I feel trapped by my responsibilities—staying in a job I hate to make credit card or mortgage payments I can barely afford—who is holding me hostage? If I'm honest with myself, the gun held to my head is in my own hand. No one is forcing me. I have chosen to do this to myself. I can own my choices or try to blame fate for them.

Everything comes back to the choices I make. These choices begin with my thoughts and attitudes and then reveal themselves in my behaviors.

In chapter four, we described discretionary effort (Principle Three) and the fact that it is about choosing to volunteer our very best, no matter the work in which or the people with whom we're involved. Principle Seven (look in the mirror first—be accountable) builds on Principle Three. If I recognize the importance of choosing to give my best effort, I begin to own my role in either succeeding or failing at what I do.

When I adopt an attitude of choosing to volunteer discretionary effort, I accept accountability for my choices and their impact, including my own happiness. Our founding fathers were onto something when they sought to guarantee the *pursuit* of happiness—not happiness itself. We each have the right to seek success. The achievement is up to us.

That's a lesson my father sought to teach me at an early age. In my community, the only swimming pool nearby was one that required membership. It wasn't expensive by today's standards ($20 per person for the summer), but it was much more than my parents were able to spend for my brother and me. Many of my friends' parents gave them the money for the membership. That seemed unfair to me. I felt cheated, as if I was entitled to something that I felt everyone else had been given. In reality, my parents hadn't said I couldn't join; they just weren't going to pay for it.

My grandparents sought to bring the pool membership within our reach. They'd pay half. Initially, I expected that my father would make up the difference. Instead, he required that we raise the other $10 ourselves. That still felt unfair. Finally, given no other options, I found odd jobs to earn my share. In the end, the compromise worked for all of us. If I really wanted to join, it became my responsibility to earn it. In the end, I valued the membership more—and even felt a sense of achievement—because I had earned it myself. I had chosen to go after it and had succeeded. I had found within myself the answer to the challenge. The lesson my father taught me is the value of ownership and the danger of entitlement.

It taught me that worrying about what my friends had, feeling as if "fairness" meant having what they had, got me nowhere. **Taking hold of my choices and grabbing the opportunity to earn what I wanted increased my self-esteem and happiness.**

As a parent, I've seen this truth borne out in my own sons. I thought I was doing the right thing in giving my middle son a car. I think it's a generational thing; we want our kids to have more than we had. What gets us into trouble is that we want them to have more, but we don't necessarily want it to be given to them.

I am still learning this lesson. That car was in beautiful condition when I presented it to my son five years ago. He has done little to maintain its appearance, and the many dents and scratches attest to that. Soon after that, my youngest son wanted a jet ski and came to me with half of the money raised. Today, it shines and runs like new. He works hard to keep it that way. For me, the difference is the level of ownership each feels toward his vehicle. (By the way, my youngest son and I both have learned a lesson here: He recognizes that things aren't given to him; I realize that he's better off for that.)

The memory of my son's car haunts me most when I look in the mirror. I complain about the car every time I see it. But when I ask myself, "What did I do to contribute to that?" I am struck by a blinding flash of the obvious. I made a choice to teach him that I'd give him what he needed with no strings attached (i.e., no expectations regarding care of the vehicle), rather than support his efforts to get those things for himself. When I am unhappy with my son's sense of entitlement, I must also hold myself accountable for it.

Happily, my middle son has matured into someone we are both extremely proud of. He is earning his own way now and not only recognizes the value of accountability but actively accepts it. He has purchased equipment that he uses to earn a living and maintains it well. He even takes better care of his car.

As a parent, my choices not only determine what I can achieve but have a profound impact on my children's ability to succeed at their goals. This ripple effect takes place not only in my household but throughout my life—at work and in my community.

In its simplest form, **we can define accountability as having to "own" one's choices, actions, outcomes, and consequences**. In other words, when something in which I was involved went well, being accountable meant that I asked the question, "How did I contribute to that success?" Likewise, when something in my life did not go well, I needed to ask the question, "How did I contribute to that not going well?"

Even when change comes from places outside our control—when there is a shift in the stock market, or when something catastrophic happens to us—**each of us is accountable for how we respond to that change.** Do we give up and complain, or are we resilient and bounce back? If I am in a leadership position, I am accountable not only to myself but to those on my team and in my organization.

An executive I coach has experienced this firsthand. His industry has taken some big hits this year, and there have been some major changes at his company. Through it all, this executive has remained optimistic. The key to his resilience has been his willingness to embrace his own accountability for what happens next.

"It's really easy when change happens," he says. "It's easy to behave as a victim. Principle Seven reminds me to look in the mirror and say 'change is coming; what more can I do to make sure it is the kind of change that is good for all of us, for the greater good as well as for me? Did I do everything I could to be prepared and prevent the worst?'

"Human capital is our most important resource, so the big mistake that we want to prevent is losing key people—really productive people who live our values, have the right skill sets and knowledge base, and who have the wisdom we need to succeed."

The words "look in the mirror first—be accountable" were deliberately chosen to convey the message that I need to be proactive in my life, recognizing that, moment-to-moment, I am making choices that determine what I can achieve and how I can help or hinder others' achievements. Each of these choices contributes to our success or failure. **The self-aware person recognizes that accountability begins with one's thinking, one's attitude, and one's beliefs.**

As we write this, the country is mired in debt and sinking deeper, while making the choices to bail out the banking and automobile industries. Whether or not this is a good decision, I'll leave to the politicians and economists. My concern is the lesson this teaches. Unless we find a way to hold accountable the business leaders whose decisions created these messes, we risk encouraging a culture of victimhood and entitlement. We undermine those who embrace accountability and hope to build not only for their own success but for the welfare of their companies and communities.

My point here is the many direct and indirect ways we teach the lessons of victimhood and entitlement. If we continue to reward business leaders whose decisions put thousands of jobs at risk with generous bonuses and bail out their companies as well, we reinforce undesired behavior. We encourage and even reward a lack of accountability with the assurance that someone else will clean up the mess. Unfortunately, this sends a discouraging message to those willing to be accountable for their own successes and failures: perhaps they needn't have worked so hard in the first place.

It would be a mistake to wait for any of these bailed-out executives to accept accountability for the failures of their companies. For a leader to look in the mirror requires that s/he be humanistic and not egocentric. The humanistic leader that we defined with Principle Two is prepared to accept accountability and be open to owning his/her mistakes. Egocentric leaders have great difficulty with that. They consider themselves victims, whether of market conditions or just bad luck. Their egocentricity blinds them from seeing what they've done or failed to do to create the conditions that exist.

Accountability is a larger and more far-reaching concept than responsibility. Actually, responsibility is a subset of accountability. It is important to be responsible, to accept the work that I have been assigned and see that it's completed per the expectations that have been established. In the workplace, responsibility lives within the bounds of my job description. Accountability, on the other hand, goes beyond owning my job responsibilities. **Accountability begins with an attitude of ownership** that becomes translated into behavior that conveys the message that I am an owner of my company (whether I legally own it or not). I have chosen to work for this organization, and I am willing to volunteer discretionary effort to see it succeed.

As a leader, it's important to model accountable behaviors for those on your team, even when it means admitting that you've made mistakes.

This can be especially challenging when the team you lead is full of hard-charging, success-driven attorneys. One of my clients, Clark, who leads such a team, is accustomed to success. Most of the attorneys working for him are brash, young males, who are confident in believing that they are on the right track. As he works through the Ten Principles, Clark is coming to realize that his usual, one-size-fits-all approach to leadership doesn't leave much room for separate realities (and is nearly always judgmental). An event the day before we conducted his interview brought him face-to-face with this truth.

"Yesterday, a woman who reports to me came in to submit her resignation. Unfortunately, she didn't work out in this role. There have been lots of folks who have been unhappy with the way she has done her job. The good news is that she's very capable in other areas and is moving onto a position that has greater responsibility than my own.

"As I think about why she hasn't succeeded here, I have to admit that there is a lot that I didn't do to help her. Clearly, I didn't start asking questions about my own contribution to her failure until it was far too late. Therefore, it wasn't something I could save. Now she is leaving on favorable terms, in part because when we talked, I admitted to her that I had really let her down. There were things I could have done to have helped her be more successful. I told her, 'I'll do better next time.'

"She felt badly treated by the guys on my team. Instead of starting with what my guys could have done differently, I started with myself and looked at my contribution to this situation."

What differentiates a high-performing team from an average-performing team is that, on a high-performing team, each member is committed to the success of the others. This is the true spirit of accountability.

If I am the chief information officer for the company, I am responsible for making sure the systems and computers are running efficiently and securely. I am probably not responsible for keeping the hallways clean or greeting visitors. Yet, if I am an accountable person—whether I'm an executive or a technician—I'll stop to pick up the piece of trash I see on the floor of the hallway; I'll greet and offer to assist the person who enters the building with me and needs help finding his/her way.

I have a neighbor who provides a shining example of this. As a retiree, he keeps in shape by running with a partner each morning. They run, side by side, along country roads, regardless of the weather. As much as I admire my neighbor for remaining fit, it's what happens as they run that makes me proud to know him. Rather than simply running past the debris people toss from cars—paper bags, beer bottles, fast-food wrappers—he and his buddy slow to a walk and clean up the roadside. They pick up the trash and dispose of it carefully.

There are probably dozens of people who see these two men running each day. Few realize, though some are taking note, that these runners not only enjoy the scenery but actively protect it. Some of those who do notice have found ways to show their appreciation. My neighbor tells me that people along his path come out with cookies to thank them for their efforts.

The value of accountability holds true at home as much as at work and in the community. In a highly functional family, each person is committed to helping the others achieve success and happiness. For parents, this requires a great deal of effort. It is much harder to help a child achieve than it is to provide what the child wants. It can be exhausting to teach a child to tie her own shoes or encourage him to keep his own room clean. Yet the return on that investment of effort is far greater, not only for the parent but especially for the child!

When we all accept accountability and ownership for our households, communities, and the organizations for which we work, we open the door to being much happier—individually and collectively. It is one more way that accountability has its roots in humanism. When I am humanistic, I recognize and embrace my "connectedness" to those around me, and I want to help them succeed with me.

Additionally, the accountable person uses his/her energy in a positive way to prevent something undesired from occurring or to find permanent solutions to problems. Using our energy to whine, complain, and moan about what should have been or about how we've been victimized simply sends us spiraling downward; we choose to be victims.

People who choose to be victims are the "energy zappers" in this world. **Accountable people are energy builders, because they inspire others.** They are humanistic and not egocentric. **They are willing to look in the mirror and admit mistakes, and they look to learn from them.** They are positive role models. They volunteer discretionary effort constantly. The focus is on progress and continuous improvement and not on perfection.

It can be easy to slip away from accountability. When someone or something has not met our expectations, there are two key questions to ask ourselves that will keep us on track:

- How did I contribute to that?
- What more will I do next time to make him/her (or it) successful?

As leaders—and, at home, as parents—we have two roles to play when it comes to accountability. We demonstrate through our actions that we accept ownership for our choices and their outcomes. Our willingness to nurture accountability in those we lead provides an equally useful lesson.

One powerful lesson we need to teach is that "doing nothing is doing something." I first learned this lesson years ago from the author and behaviorist, Dr. Aubrey C. Daniels. **When we fail to address undesired behavior, we positively reinforce it.** When I overlook inappropriate humor or even sarcasm in the workplace, I reinforce it; I send the message that it is acceptable behavior. This not only encourages undesired behavior, but it undermines accountability among others on the team, who begin to wonder why they are offering discretionary effort and working to live the Ten Principles. Gradually, the weight of the negative example will sink the team.

As you remember, the Ten Principles build on one another. It takes Principles One through Six to skillfully model accountable behavior. For example, when I'm in the moment, I recognize the negative impact of undesired behavior, such as sarcasm. I make time to approach the individual and, with authenticity and humanism, discuss it with him/her. Because I value discretionary effort, I get past my own discomfort and accept responsibility for having that sensitive conversation. In doing so, I illustrate or model behavior that will benefit him or her, as well as the team. I am open to the team member's separate reality and listen with curiosity. In the end, though, I hold myself accountable as a leader and work with the team member on improving his/her behavior. At the end of the day, my accountability helps everyone succeed.

Principle Seven Review: Look in the mirror first—be accountable.

- There is only one person I can control and change; that person is *me*. I am in control of the choices I make and the consequences I experience.
- When I adopt an attitude of choosing to give discretionary effort, I accept accountability for my choices and their impact, including my own happiness.

- We can define accountability as choosing to "own" one's thoughts, actions, outcomes, and consequences.
- When change occurs, each of us is accountable for how we respond to that change.
- The self-aware person recognizes that accountability begins with one's thinking and one's attitude and is translated into one's behavior.
- Accountability begins with an "attitude of ownership."
- What differentiates a high-performing team from an average-performing team is that, on a high-performing team, each member is committed to the success of the others. This is the true spirit of accountability.
- Accountable people are energy builders because they inspire others. They are humanistic and not egocentric. They are willing to look in the mirror, to admit mistakes, and to learn from them.

Moving from being accountable, the next chapter focuses on reaching out to others and having courageous conversations. This also ties into an authentic and humanistic approach to dealing with conflict and other challenging situations—at work and at home.

Look in the Mirror First—Be Accountable: Personal Reflection

1. When things do not go as hoped at work, where does your thinking go first? Be honest with yourself.

    _____
    _____
    _____
    _____

2. Do you tend to assign blame to things or others, or do you first ask yourself, "How did I contribute to that?" and "What more will I do next time to make it successful?"

    _____
    _____
    _____
    _____

3. Which of the Ten Principles do you need to fully employ in order to look first at your personal accountability for your negative result(s)?

    _____
    _____
    _____
    _____

4. Are there situations in which, or people with whom, you're doing nothing (perhaps to avoid conflict) when you should be doing something—e.g., providing constructive (i.e., corrective) feedback and coaching? What message are you conveying?

    _____
    _____
    _____
    _____

5. How do these same questions apply at home? How does this impact your relationships and happiness? What will you do to repair these relationships?

    _____

    _____

    _____

    _____

Be accountable now!

Chapter Nine

Principle Eight: Have Courageous Conversations

. . . .

"Courage is what it takes to stand up and speak; courage is also what it takes to sit down and listen."

Anonymous

The only thing necessary for the triumph of evil is for good men to do nothing."

Edmund Burke

"Let me assert my firm belief that the only thing we have to fear is fear itself."

Franklin Delano Roosevelt

At this moment, the news is full of layoffs and bankruptcies. The scariest question is, "Am I next?" No one wants to ask it out loud, though.

So here's another question: "What is the worst that could happen if I do ask?"

If I am afraid about my future, I am undeniably distracted from getting my job done right the first time, even more so from offering discretionary effort. Looked at coldly, if I'm preoccupied with worry and fear, I'm actually putting myself at greater risk. If I remember Principle Seven and ask what more can I do to improve the situation, **I am ready to have a courageous conversation. I am ready to face my fear and ask**, perhaps not whether I am next but what I can do to improve the company's and my own situation. It may initially require courage, but it also makes good sense.

Courageous conversations come in all shapes and sizes. Whether I'm afraid for my future or simply sitting in a seemingly aimless meeting, wondering what it is we all expect to accomplish, I am often held back by my own sense of insecurity from asking questions that are gnawing at me. I may wonder, "Who am I to ask that question? Am I the only one in the dark here? Will I look foolish if I do ask?"

The hidden truth is that I'm probably not alone. As soon as I say, "This may sound like a stupid question, but I'm unclear what it is we're trying to achieve," I routinely find that others share my concern. All it took to clear the air was for one person to speak up. How often do we come to realize that truth? How often do we dodge our accountability for our own lack of understanding and participation, by remaining silent?

There is an exercise I do with clients. The executives are sitting at tables in teams, and each team is given a set of puzzle pieces and asked to assemble equal-size squares—one for each member of the team. I provide a simple set of instructions, and in no time, the teams jump to work. Some teams struggle mightily and require coaching to complete their squares. Others struggle a bit but eventually build equal-size squares. In twenty years of playing the "Broken Squares Game," no one has ever stopped me at the outset of the game to ask the most basic question: "How big should the equal-size squares be?"

When we debrief and discuss this, the players tell me that they were certain that others at their table had the answer and that they were alone in their confusion or that they assumed it would become clear as the game progressed. Rather than seeking clarity and risking exposing what they didn't know, they soldiered on and did the best they could with limited understanding. Eventually, they completed the squares, but look at how much time was lost because *the* most important question went unasked at the beginning of the game?

The way that people play the "Broken Square Game" mirrors what often happens in the real world at work and at home. Given this reality, I ask all executives with whom I work to launch a "Raise Your Hand" campaign in their workplaces. In other words, when someone doesn't understand something, when someone makes a mistake, when someone disagrees, or when someone has a different solution that s/he believes might work, encourage him/her to be accountable and raise his/her hand. Saying, "I humbly disagree; have you considered this alternative?" is empowering and far more productive than unexpressed or inappropriately expressed frustration. *Silence is the enemy within* that plagues many companies today. Therefore, business executives must create an organizational culture that drives out fear and encourages and rewards courageous conversations. That is the culture that can remain resilient and rise to a challenge.

A courageous conversation requires that I engage and say what I honestly think and feel to whom and when I need to say it, in a humanistic manner, so that others can hear my message without feeling judged and respond to it in like manner without feeling afraid.

Without courageous conversations, valuable time, energy, and productivity—$$$—are wasted because of what goes unsaid in meetings and in other human interactions where honesty, direction, expectations, clarity, and/or feedback are desperately needed but not delivered. Obviously, business execution and performance suffer when people fail to have courageous conversations.

What people often forget is that without Principles One through Seven working in harmony, they cannot effectively execute Principle Eight—let alone Principles Nine and Ten. Each principle is an essential piece of a powerful leadership model. When even one piece is neglected, we do not perform at our very best, and we do not have the positive impact we desire on relationships and results.

Over time, we've come to realize that courageous conversations represent one of the most misunderstood and misapplied leadership principles. This is so, in part, because people interpret "courageous" to mean that they have permission to tell people what they really think of them (i.e., "let them have it") without regard for how or when the message is delivered or how it might be received. Obviously, when operating under this interpretation of a courageous conversation, it should not be surprising that one or more of the preceding seven principles is often left out. Though some are easier to apply than others, all are equally important and interdependent.

Here's a quick review of the two principles that are most often ignored or misapplied when having a courageous conversation.

Principle One: Be in the moment. In order to have a healthy, productive courageous conversation, I need to be completely in the moment. I need to give my undivided attention to the person(s) with whom I am interacting. At home, in meetings, and in other forums where I interact with others, I can sometimes fail to be fully present and can engage in what I've called autopilot behavior. Examples of autopilot behavior could be rolling my eyes when someone says something I disagree with, blurting out an inappropriate comment when I am frustrated, or working on my BlackBerry when I get bored in a meeting. In psychological terms, being on autopilot is moving habitually and quickly from stimulus to reaction (S→R) without pausing in between to consider and choose an appropriate response.

The bottom line is that, for a courageous conversation to have its most positive impact, it must occur when I can be and remain in the moment. Being in the moment enables me to be more self-aware so I can access and push the pause button when necessary, to allow me to be thoughtful and choose a more appropriate response. Being in the moment also enables me to access my inner wisdom, so I can readily share personal feelings, observations, and comments that can elevate the quality of the interaction. *We have the makings of a courageous conversation when we choose to share our personal thoughts, feelings, observations, etc., in a meeting or one-on-one exchange, and elect to do so in a humanistic manner.*

Principle Two: Be authentic and humanistic. The authentic side of this principle is relatively self-explanatory. When I choose to have a courageous conversation, I need to be honest and say what I truly feel, without putting what's on my mind on the back burner for too long. That said, when and how I communicate my feelings are vitally important for courageous conversations to be effective. In discussing Principle One, we talked about the "when." Let's now address the "how."

This is where the second part of Principle Two, being humanistic, comes into play. Unfortunately, it is this part that many people seem to misinterpret or leave out when having courageous conversations. *When I am humanistic while having a courageous conversation, I care about two important things: 1) being respectful and maintaining or enhancing the self-esteem of the person(s) with whom I am interacting, and 2) achieving a positive outcome to the conversation.*

Remember our definition of a courageous conversation, one in which I "engage and say what I honestly think and feel to whom and when I need to say it, in a humanistic manner, so that others can hear my message without feeling judged and respond to it in like manner without feeling afraid." If I undertake to have a courageous conversation with you (for example, providing constructive feedback on a sensitive issue), as a humanistic person I take care to leave you feeling respected, feeling that your self-esteem is whole or intact. I *must* approach these conversations with humility and curiosity—not judgment. As a result, you are more likely to act on the feedback and accept my recommendation to improve your behavior. What's more, the relationship between us remains respectful and productive.

One of the executives I coach has made courageous conversations the norm among members of her team. "We have changed the dynamics of the leadership team when it comes to raising concerns or issues. It's no longer okay to sit quietly and act as if you agree when you really don't. We all have a responsibility to speak up, especially at the executive level. We need to own what happens here."

This isn't easy for everyone, of course. Many people, even leaders, are accustomed to avoiding conflict. One leader with whom we've worked worries that his colleagues have come to think of him as too much of a "nice guy"; he acknowledges that this can "work to my detriment as a leader." For him, recognizing the importance of being humanistic when having courageous conversations—i.e., leaving those he deals with feeling respected—has made all the difference. He now sees that **being authentic as a leader means accepting accountability for the well-being of the team and the achievement of its goals, and being more assertive.**

This holds true not only in the workplace but also at home. There may be no other job more important or challenging than parenting. In the role of parent, behaving accountably and being willing to initiate courageous conversations with our children is essential for their success. The child whose inappropriate behavior goes unchecked is poorly prepared for what life has to offer. Part of being a parent is taking on responsibility for teaching one's children to understand that their actions and their behaviors have an impact on the world and the people in it. It is every bit as important to approach the challenges of parenting in a humanistic way—to leave the child's self-esteem intact.

It is important to note that not every courageous conversation involves constructive feedback or correcting a child's behavior. Sometimes it takes more courage to simply be vulnerable, speak up, and expose one of your own weaknesses. If I admit to my children that I've made a mistake, I model accountable behavior for them. In the future, perhaps they will be more likely to have similar courageous conversations with me.

When we allow important things to go unsaid—whether in meetings or in our personal lives—we sacrifice authenticity. At some level, we become less trustworthy. Think about what is lost in terms of relationships, because we choose not to ask or say what is truly on our minds.

Finally, how much happier would we be if we gave ourselves permission to ask questions and to begin courageous conversations with one another? If you're like me, the fear and insecurity that used to cause me to not speak up in relationships and in meetings doomed me to a life of worry and self-imposed frustration. The Ten Principles have taught me how to be authentic and how to say what I need to say in a humanistic manner, so the impact I have on others can be positive no matter what the content of the message. I have found that the Ten Principles pave the way for personal satisfaction and happiness if I choose to follow them.

Principle Eight Review: Have courageous conversations.

- A courageous conversation requires that I engage and say what I honestly think and feel to whom and when I need to say it, in a humanistic manner, so that others can hear my message without feeling judged and respond to it in like manner without being afraid.
- Being authentic as a leader means accepting accountability for initiating and participating in courageous conversations.
- When we allow important things to go unsaid—whether in personal relationships or in the workplace—we sacrifice authenticity. At some level, we become less trustworthy.

In the next chapter, we move on to Principle Nine: Provide timely, clear, and specific performance expectations and feedback. This will build on the previous eight principles and move you toward achieving peak performance.

HAVE COURAGEOUS CONVERSATIONS: PERSONAL REFLECTION

1. What courageous conversations do you need to have at work? When will you have them? How can you use the earlier principles to improve the outcomes of those conversations?

   _____

   _____

   _____

   _____

2. Are there certain situations where you avoid having courageous conversations? What do you stand to gain by opening up and sharing? What, if anything, do you stand to lose by remaining silent?

   _____

   _____

   _____

   _____

3. Are there certain people with whom you avoid having courageous conversations? Why? What is your thinking? How will you change your thinking and behavior?

   _____

   _____

   _____

   _____

4. How do these same questions apply to your home life?

   _____

   _____

   _____

   _____

5. What are the payoffs (in your relationships and results) when you choose to have needed courageous conversations?

   _____

   _____

   _____

   _____

6. With whom will you have a needed courageous conversation? When?

_____
_____
_____
_____

Be accountable now!

Chapter Ten

Principle Nine: Provide Timely, Clear, and Specific Performance Expectations and Feedback

• •

"Doing nothing is doing something to performance."

Aubrey C. Daniels

"Each of us does, in effect, strike a series of deals or compromises between the wants and longings of the inner self and an outer environment that offers certain possibilities and sets certain limitations."

Maggie Scarf

Why have rules? What's the point?

Each night, the news is full of stories of people living outside the law or failing to follow the basic norms of behavior expected of each of us in society. We are subtly encouraged to focus on what's wrong with our world. We focus on those who deviate, who don't abide by the rules. For many of us, this leads to depressing thoughts—not to happy ones!

So what about the vast majority of people who live law-abiding, responsible lives? We forget that the vast majority of our neighbors, coworkers, and fellow parents at our kids' schools are living thoughtful, caring lives and trying their best to do the right thing.

Think about this. In this country, we have 300 million people, who are each living a separate reality. As you recall, each of us sees life through our unique set of lenses or filters, shaped by life experiences and our beliefs, and each of us typically believes that his/her personal reality is the best reality. Said differently, each of these 300 million people's behavior makes sense to him/her—perhaps not to us, but certainly to him/her. Given this, without rules or laws (i.e., expectations) and consequences governing how we behave in society, we would have chaos. Each of us would operate according to our own needs, regardless of the impact on others. When I think of this, post-apocalyptic movies like *Mad Max* come to mind. It isn't a world I'd like to try to survive in, much less one I'd hope to succeed in.

The bottom line is this: Without expectations first, followed by consequences, life would be chaotic.

At LeadQuest, we define high performance (HP) as being equal to desired results (DR) plus desired behaviors (DB); $HP = DR + DB$. The achievement of high performance begins with defining the desired results and desired behaviors. We call these performance expectations.

Setting performance expectations is the starting point for achieving success (desired results through desired behaviors). Most, if not all, organizations have what is called a performance management system or process. The performance management process is comprised of three major components:

1. *Setting performance expectations,* comprised of desired results and desired behaviors (technical and interpersonal behaviors like the Ten Principles), normally occurs on an annual basis at the beginning of the organization's performance year. Performance expectations need to be SMART (specific, measurable, agreed upon, realistic, and time bound).
2. *Observing and measuring performance* related to these expectations.
3. *Delivering feedback:* informal feedback during the year as well as formal feedback as part of what is typically called an end-of-year performance review.

Feedback is information, delivered as the job is being performed or soon after, on how well expectations are being met. When a task is completed successfully, feedback describes the specific results and behaviors that led to that success. When a project is unfinished or does not succeed, feedback addresses the specific steps that were not taken, or that were taken incorrectly, and the behaviors that caused the undesired performance. Timing is key.

The most powerful consequences, such as feedback, are those that are delivered as the person is performing or shortly thereafter. At LeadQuest, we have what we call the Twenty-Four-Hour Rule (i.e., all feedback must be delivered within twenty-four hours of observing performance). By doing so, the person to whom we deliver the feedback is more likely to remember the specifics of what happened.

When we look at our daily lives, we do amazingly well. I board an airplane, confident that the pilot is highly skilled and dedicated to carrying my fellow passengers and me safely to our destination. When I drive down the highway, I stay between the lines and trust that other drivers will do the same. We understand what is expected of us, and we satisfy those expectations. Using the law as our standard, we hold ourselves accountable for our own safety and for the safety of others.

When I forget or am careless, there are built-in, gentle reminders (i.e., feedback) that have been put in place by some kind person I'll never know. If I start the car and begin driving without having fastened my seatbelt, a bell sounds. If I veer onto the shoulder of the highway, it's brought to my attention as I feel and hear the tires riding on the rumble strip. That instant feedback is all I need to get back on track and succeed at my task—driving safely. If I go without an accident, my insurance carrier might reward me with a lower premium!

We are at our best when we understand what is expected of us and when we receive timely feedback that helps us stay on track; employee engagement increases when employees receive routine and timely feedback. Resilience also increases. Whether we are talking about the workplace or our personal lives, we are happiest when we communicate to help one another succeed.

In fact, success is predicated on clear expectations and timely, specific feedback.

However, no matter how clearly they are presented, expectations alone will not guarantee success. Based on research in the science of applied behavior analysis, Julie Smith, PhD, cofounder of the Continuous Learning Group, has stated that 80 percent of the impact on human behavior comes from consequences (i.e., what people experience when they behave, or shortly thereafter, that makes it more or less likely that they will behave that way again), such as appreciative and constructive feedback. To increase the likelihood that people will meet performance expectations, they must know that there will be consequences (positive or negative) for their actions, that they will receive feedback or other consequences for their performance in a timely fashion. Highly accountable leaders consistently deliver appropriate consequences when performance expectations are met or not met.

In my workshops, I ask this question: "Suppose you knew that someone had information that would help you be even more successful in your job, but they chose not to share it with you. How would you feel?" The common, even overwhelming response is, "I'd feel cheated."

Then I ask, "So, how many of you have information that you could share right now with coworkers in this room that would help them improve and be even more successful?" Almost all hands go up.

When I ask, "Have you shared it?," most people say no!

The contradiction is obvious. Most of us would feel cheated if others withheld feedback; yet few of us are willing to offer it. Why is this?

When I pose this question in the workshop, participants say they are uncomfortable offering constructive (i.e., corrective) feedback. They say they are afraid of how the feedback will be received. It might lead to conflict. They assume that the feedback they deliver will be seen as harsh criticism, even when they intend for it to be helpful.

The key is to provide the feedback in a way that increases the likelihood that the person will be able to hear and then act on the feedback—i.e., s/he will see it as helpful and not harmful. When you take the time to offer constructive feedback, using the principles and keeping the other person's feelings in mind, your feedback will be helpful and received positively.

Let's be clear. There are times when disciplinary action is called for and a leader needs to step up and take decisive action for the good of the organization. Certain things, such as sexual harassment and racism, cannot be tolerated in the workplace. Employees who continue to fall short of expectations or who violate organizational policies after they have been coached/counseled should be moved out of the organization—sooner rather than later.

Even in these extreme cases, *how* you deliver the message is extremely important. It should be constructive, with an eye toward helping the employee see how to be successful in his/her next job in a different company. True leadership upholds the values of the organization in every interaction. There is no room here for destructive behavior, for the old "an eye for an eye, a tooth for a tooth" paradigm.

In most cases, however, when an employee makes a mistake, the employee can learn from that mistake and become a more valuable contributor to the team. This is where it is important to understand the true meaning of constructive feedback. Constructive feedback has *building* as its goal. The employee should feel that s/he is being treated with respect. While it is made clear that a mistake was made, the steps that can be taken to correct the mistake—and to make a fresh start—are made equally clear. And, all of this is accomplished in a humanistic way.

A successful leader creates an environment in which it is safe to learn from one's mistakes. The leader who delivers only negative consequences, without accepting any personal accountability for the behavior of his/her team members, creates an environment of fear. When we learn that our mistakes can only hurt us and that we have no opportunity to recover from them, we learn that it is foolish to try. Or worse, we resort to desperate measures—such as lying about or hiding our mistakes or blaming others for them. The leader who fails to understand the impact of constructive feedback in building trust, in improving performance, and in strengthening the resilience of the team undermines the team and organization.

The Ten Principles were inspired by my belief in leadership accountability. As such, they are a useful resource for guiding leaders in creating confident, resilient teams. When we take the time and are mindful of the eight principles leading up to Principle Nine, we understand how to offer feedback so that it can be welcomed and utilized. Remember how we define Principle Eight: A courageous conversation requires that I engage and say what I honestly think and feel to whom and when I need to say it, in a humanistic manner, so that others can hear my message without feeling judged and respond to it in like manner without feeling afraid. At the end of the day, **the goal of constructive feedback is for others to receive the message positively and then act upon it immediately to make the necessary improvements.** This requires focusing on "the what" (the content of the feedback) and "the how" (the way the feedback is delivered).

One client of mine, a hospital CFO, is making progress with an employee whose behavior created conflict. When he undertook a new function at his organization, Dave inherited the team that had been in place. One employee, in particular, exhibited some problematic behaviors that undermined the success of the team.

"By focusing on Principle Nine and by being very clear and very structured in the way that I set expectations and provided feedback, I've been able to move an employee to a point where we are beginning to see some turnaround. I think there is an opportunity for continued behavioral improvement that has resulted from the use of Principle Nine.

"You have to be prepared to leverage the other eight principles, but it works. The structure of the principles—and the fact that they're grounded in behavioral and communication science—has given me the confidence to be very direct and do so in a way that is not threatening to the other person. This is powerful!"

The value of thoughtful feedback holds true in all relationships, not just in those in which there is a leader and a follower or a boss and an employee. For me, the classic example of this principle is found in most marriage vows. Traditional marriage vows clearly spell out what is hoped of the couple and what each should expect from the other. Yet, who would dream that reciting a set of promises in a ceremony would be enough? It is the day-to-day expression of love and support—and the day-to-day negotiation (or renegotiation) of expectations and the timely delivery of feedback—that holds a couple together.

Because my work requires so much travel, I hold myself accountable for the things that go on outside our home (e.g., lawn care and house maintenance) and depend on my wife to manage our household. We understand our roles and are ready to do our parts. That isn't really enough, though. When I let my wife know how wonderful it feels to come home to a calm, well-ordered household, not only do I give her appreciative feedback, but I also remind myself of the immeasurable value she brings to my life. When she lets me know that she understands the challenges of my work and acknowledges the energy that it requires, I know that I am appreciated. When either of us is distracted by our individual challenges and operates on autopilot, it's easy to take the other's contribution for granted. If it goes on long enough, feeling unappreciated can give way to resentment and anger. In a successful, happy marriage, it takes both partners to recognize this and to communicate well with one another.

Probably because of the work I do and the behavioral science I've studied, I introduced feedback into our marriage in a very purposeful way. On at least a quarterly basis, my wife and I go out to dinner—just us, no kids, no cooking—and an evening of relaxation and conversation. The conversation includes what has become known as the "napkin exercise." We touch on each aspect of our marriage (the list includes communication, respect and support, personal growth, financial management, parenting, and sex) and assign it a rating. We each write down the rating, using a ten-point scale (with ten being the highest score), hold up the napkin to compare results and begin to talk about the thought behind each one. It leads to wonderful conversation and does a lot to help us understand one another's changing needs and expectations (i.e., separate realities). The feedback causes us to make the necessary adjustments to keep our marriage current and vibrant.

Once a year, we extend this conversation to include our sons and their significant others. Each Thanksgiving weekend, we hold a "State of the Family" meeting. We begin by looking back over the previous year, recalling what we want to celebrate—individual and family successes. Next, we talk about individual and family opportunities for improvement. At the core of this yearly ritual is the appreciative and constructive feedback that we offer one another. Early on in this process, I learned that I needed to set the right example by soliciting both types of feedback from my family. *Accountable leaders don't sit back and wait for wanted feedback, they routinely solicit it.*

The State of the Family meeting typically runs for two to three hours and helps us form personal and family goals for the upcoming year. Even as my boys have grown and begun to launch their own lives, we talk almost daily.

In our conversations, we constantly solicit feedback from and offer feedback to each other. Our annual ritual has the additional benefit of focusing the feedback that we provide one another during those ongoing conversations.

It's only fair to point out that this wasn't received warmly on the first few tries. Our boys called it "hokey" and "group therapy," and they groused about having a meeting. Now, they are ready participants, helping us and one another to reach goals that matter to us.

In his book *Bringing out the Best in People,* Aubrey C. Daniels, PhD, cites research that indicates **the average human being needs to hear four times as many pieces of appreciative feedback as constructive feedback to stay motivated and volunteer discretionary effort in meeting performance expectations**. This is known as the Four-to-One Rule.

When I give seminars and ask participants what ratio of appreciative to constructive feedback they deliver to their significant others, I often hear one-to-four or even one-to-ten! I follow that question up by asking what the impact of that is on the health and happiness of their relationships. Not surprisingly, I hear agreement that the relationships would be better off if the ratio were more in line with the Four-to-One Rule. Sadly, some people feel uncomfortable delivering appreciative feedback, or they assume that their partner doesn't need to hear it. When we can bring the first eight principles into alignment and apply the Four-to-One Rule, we are not only better prepared to deliver appreciative feedback but also more comfortable receiving it.

One physician leader with whom I work says his profession is particularly unaccustomed to giving appreciative feedback. "As physicians, we're trained to see what's wrong. We seldom recognize what's right, so feedback tends to be critical; it tends to be about what's wrong.

"But I've seen how helpful it is to show we appreciate when someone is doing good work. I'm working on Principle Nine. It's still a challenge for me."

So why are we reluctant to give and accept appreciative feedback, even in the workplace? What core belief is getting in the way of us praising someone who has done well, who has met our expectations? Just as important to ask: What core belief is getting in the way of us accepting appreciative feedback? After all, don't we recognize our accountability for the success of the team?

Many of us have grown up suspicious of compliments. We learned first that we don't deserve them and then that the person paying the compliment might have some hidden agenda and should not be trusted. But is that really true most of the time? When you attend a wonderful concert, don't you applaud? So when someone does something well, why are we reluctant to tell him/her?

In reality, more appreciative feedback is sorely needed in most organizations with which I've worked. If we understand the impact of the Four-to-One Rule, we realize that recognizing good work with specific and timely feedback not only reinforces the desired behavior and results, but it also illustrates our commitment to the expectations we have presented. Then, when we must offer constructive feedback to tell someone how they could produce even better results through better behaviors, we have greater credibility.

The physician quoted above has a structured way to keep himself on track as he works on this principle. He keeps a record—a logbook—of his interactions and indicates each time he has provided feedback, noting to whom he offered it and whether it was appreciative or constructive. He has found it a helpful way to hold himself accountable, over time, to delivering more frequent feedback.

It is equally important to be mindful of how we accept appreciative feedback. If someone praises work you have done or the way you have done it, **listening to what is being said and accepting the feedback strengthens your relationship and demonstrates your understanding of the importance of the work you've done.** Shrugging it off or, worse, denying that you have earned it is both ungracious and insulting. A good rule of thumb to follow is this: In most cases, a sincere "Thank you" is eloquent enough.

This principle also applies in a significant way to parenting. How many of you routinely set expectations for your children only to become disappointed when they are not met? Holding yourself accountable, what has been your contribution to that result? Remember, expectations that are not stated clearly, checked for understanding, and agreed upon, and that do not hold guaranteed consequences (e.g., appreciative feedback or punishment, such as grounding) are less likely to be met successfully. A common expectation is that a child will keep his/her room clean. So many parents, upon finding a messy room, resort to yelling, which amounts to little more than restating an expectation in a much louder voice.

The parent who praises a child for having put clean clothes into the dresser and dirty ones in the hamper and for putting toys and books back where they belong—or who restricts a child's freedom until those chores have been completed—is not only providing clear expectations but also accepting his/her responsibility for the child's success by providing appropriate consequences. Moreover, the parent is providing the child with a key lesson needed to succeed in life. The earlier this starts in life, the better. But you can, indeed, teach an old dog new tricks. If you learn behavior, you can unlearn it and break a bad habit; of course, this requires a desire to change. The good news is that you can teach yourself to provide and accept timely, specific feedback.

Earlier we learned that "doing nothing is doing something." In the previous example, the parent who neither praises the child for a clean room nor delivers negative consequences for a messy one is not only doomed to frustration but, more importantly, teaches the child that an expectation that is ignored long enough will just go away. Consequently, the child grows up believing that, as parents, we aren't paying attention to his/her worst or best work and that it is pointless to try to please us. In teaching this lesson, we are also cheating our children out of the satisfaction that comes from a job well done.

In the workplace, unsuccessful leaders have concluded that, because those on their teams are adults, expectations and feedback are no longer required. On the contrary, "doing nothing is doing something" in this setting as well. Here, employees not only learn from the consequences of their own actions but also observe and learn from those faced by others. **Tolerating poor performance by a few workers will undermine the discretionary effort of those who regularly meet expectations.**

It is important to note that good performers need to hear appreciative feedback in order to continue to give discretionary effort. Sometimes, because we are tolerating poor performance, we load more work on those who perform well. They end up feeling punished for doing good work. Those people—the ones who provide cost-effective results—become frustrated and angry. Then they leave or slack off.

Based on input from numerous chief financial officers with whom I've worked, I've learned that upward of 70 percent of all company operating expenses are consumed by employee salaries and benefits. So, when we tolerate poor performance, we are wasting money. During the current recession, when cutting expenses is paramount, paying attention to performance and delivering clear expectations and feedback can be the keys to preventing future layoffs. Let's be crystal clear. This is a leadership accountability issue. When we don't employ the Ten Principles of Personal Leadership, we set ourselves and others up for failure.

At the end of the day, expectations and feedback are rooted in accountability. At work, we create job descriptions and provide performance reviews, because we want to help the person in the job (and ourselves) succeed. That's the leader's number one job.

At home, whether it's doing the napkin exercise with your significant other or holding a State of the Family meeting, taking time to communicate with one another in this way demonstrates your belief in each person's fundamental goodness and your commitment to each other's success.

Principle Nine Review: Provide timely, clear, and specific performance expectations and feedback.

- Performance expectations define both desired results and desired behaviors.
- Performance expectations need to be SMART (specific, measurable, agreed upon, realistic, and time bound).
- Feedback is information, delivered as the job is being performed or soon after, on how well the expectations are being met.
- We are at our best when we understand what is expected of us and when we receive timely and specific feedback that helps us stay on track; employee engagement increases when employees receive frequent and helpful feedback.
- The key is to provide the feedback in a way that increases the likelihood that the person will be able to hear and act on the feedback—i.e., s/he will see it as helpful and not harmful.
- A successful leader creates an environment in which it is safe to learn from one's mistakes; a successful leader solicits feedback routinely.
- The goal of constructive feedback is for others to receive the message positively and then act upon it immediately to make the necessary improvements. This requires focusing on "the what" (the content of the feedback) and "the how" (the way the feedback is delivered).
- The average human being needs to hear four times as many pieces of appreciative feedback as constructive feedback to stay motivated and volunteer discretionary effort.
- How you receive feedback is also important. If someone praises work you have done or the way you have done it, listening to what is being said and accepting the feedback strengthens your relationship and demonstrates your willingness to receive feedback.
- Tolerating poor performance by a few workers will undermine the amount of discretionary effort volunteered by those who regularly meet expectations.
- Ultimately, soliciting and delivering expectations and feedback are rooted in accountability.

The next chapter will focus on how the Ten Principles of Personal Leadership can be applied to teaching, coaching, and mentoring others on a daily basis.

DELIVER CLEAR, TIMELY, AND SPECIFIC PERFORMANCE EXPECTATIONS AND FEEDBACK: PERSONAL REFLECTION

Think about the last major project you undertook with your team. Think back to the original assignment and the expectations and feedback you provided.

1. What went well? What tasks were performed in a way that met or exceeded your expectations? Why?

   _____
   _____
   _____
   _____

2. How clearly stated were your expectations? Did each person express understanding and agreement on what was expected? If not, why not? What was the impact of that?

   _____
   _____
   _____
   _____

3. What kind of feedback did you provide to those responsible? Did you provide feedback along the way or wait until the project was completed? What was the impact of that on the productivity of your team?

   _____
   _____
   _____
   _____

4. What didn't go well? Why? How did you hold yourself accountable?

   _____
   _____
   _____
   _____

5. What kind of feedback did you provide to those who did not meet your expectations? When did you provide it? How was it delivered and received? What was the outcome?

_____

_____

_____

_____

6. What will you do next time to ensure that your team has the tools—particularly specific and timely expectations and feedback—it needs to succeed?

_____

_____

_____

_____

Now think about the health of and level of happiness in your personal life.

7. When was the last time you and your significant other(s) talked openly about your hopes and expectations for your relationship(s)?

_____

_____

_____

_____

8. In your personal life, what is the ratio of appreciative to constructive feedback that you offer? Do you usually speak up to offer thanks or praise? Are you usually critical? What is the impact on your relationships? On your happiness?

_____

_____

_____

_____

9. What will you do right now to improve your personal relationships? To create more happiness in yourself and others?

_____

_____

_____

_____

Be accountable now!

Chapter Eleven

Principle Ten: Teach, Coach, and Mentor—Spend at least Half of Your Time Developing Others

. . . .

"The single biggest way to achieve organizational success is to focus on leadership development. There is almost no limit to the potential of an organization that recruits good people, raises them up as leaders, and continually develops them."

John C. Maxwell

"If you fail to honor your people, they will fail to honor you; it is said of a good leader that when the work is done, the aim fulfilled, the people will say, 'We did this ourselves.'"

Lao Tzu

"Be gentle, and you can be bold; be frugal, and you can be liberal; avoid putting yourself before others, and you can become a leader among men."

Lao Tzu

I know what you're thinking. "Half of my time? *Half* of my time? How much free time does this guy think I have?"

Here's the good news: I'm not suggesting you work more hours. I'm here to tell you that you're already teaching your team through virtually every interaction you have with them at work (and, for that matter, with your children at home). The real question is: Are you teaching and modeling the things that you want them to learn?

Each time you listen actively in a meeting, each time you invite fresh ideas or solicit feedback on your performance from your team and listen with curiosity rather than judgment, you are teaching by example; you are behaving accountably. As a leader, your example has extraordinary impact.

Example has more power than most people in leadership positions recognize. When you lead with intention, when you bring the previous nine principles to every interaction or task, **you will find that you are already spending not 50 percent but 100 percent of your time teaching, coaching, and mentoring.** The time you are already spending at work achieves greater purpose. In other words, if you plan to teach, coach, and mentor for even half of the time, you'll find that *all* of your interactions are more successful.

Let's be clear about what we mean by teach, coach, and mentor. These terms are interrelated and sometimes used interchangeably, but each action has its own purpose and value. **As a teacher, you are imparting your knowledge**, your wisdom, to your team or to someone on it. You have acquired the knowledge and skills required to do a job well—whether we're talking about operations or administration. You have developed the business intelligence and emotional intelligence needed to be successful. You have helpful information to share.

As a coach, you are mindful of the steps your team or family members are taking along the way. You are prepared to **instruct, direct, and even prompt them to shift focus**, to point them in a direction that will be more useful to them.

Good coaches are great listeners and observers. If you've ever worked with a golf professional, you are grateful for his/her attention to detail. A great coach can tell you with precision how to adjust your grip or your stance to hit the ball straighter, longer, etc. S/he understands the mechanics of the swing and pays close attention to yours to help you understand and improve them. *Coaching is about knowing* what should be *and paying attention to* what is *in order to provide clear direction to close the gap.* When you provide clear performance expectations and timely feedback, you are being an effective leader and coach.

As a mentor, you are a guide. You've been through this territory—or something like it—and you know the way. You've faced enough challenges to show others how they can overcome theirs. You and those you are leading share a common goal; your role is to help them see what they need to do to achieve it. Mentoring usually involves some level of teaching and coaching. We see this all the time in the workplace. A junior person is assigned to work with someone more senior for the purpose of gaining knowledge or a specific set of skills.

Think of your own childhood for a moment. No one expected you to figure out for yourself how to tie your shoes. Someone—probably more than one person—showed you how and celebrated with you when you mastered the skill. Getting it right felt wonderful. Being praised for learning something new and doing it well was life-changing.

We never truly outgrow the need to learn, grow, and celebrate along the way. That sense of accomplishment that comes with learning something new is fresh each time. So why do we think that praising someone on the team who does well, or even complimenting a teenager for good behavior, is unnecessary?

Many of us grew up believing that adults should already know what they need to know and how to behave. Adults shouldn't need direction or praise. We learned that offering appreciative feedback would lead to giving someone a big head, which becomes that person's cue to slack off. The belief operating here is that if I tell you you're doing a good job, you'll stop.

Not only does personal experience illustrate the false logic there, behavioral research—particularly the work on employee engagement that the Gallup Organization has done—has proven it wrong. In their book *12: The Elements of Great Managing,* the authors document the Gallup Organization's findings based on 10 million workplace interviews they've conducted on the subject of employee engagement. One of the questions reviewed in the book states that, to stay engaged, "In the last seven days, I [employee] have received recognition or praise for doing good work."

Remember the Four-to-One Rule from the last chapter: The average person needs to hear four times as much appreciative feedback as constructive feedback in order to stay motivated and volunteer discretionary effort. **If we hope to lead effectively, we must be prepared to offer not only constructive feedback but praise—we must celebrate achievement.** Great teachers, coaches, and mentors understand this. Not only do they offer feedback, but they regularly solicit feedback on their own performance. They behave accountably by asking questions, such as "What can I do to be even more effective?"

The false logic—the belief that praise is dangerous—drives destructive leadership behavior. Providing feedback only when correction is needed and devoting the majority of interactions to pointing out errors creates distrust and fear—both in the workplace and at home. It causes workers to conclude that a manager is impossible to please, so they stop trying. Martha Peak, as group editor for the American Management Association's *Management Review,* described the impact. "My father had a simple test that helps me measure my own leadership quotient: 'When you are out of the office,' he once asked me, 'does your staff carry on remarkably well without you?'"

There is another belief that can undermine Principle Ten: "I don't have time to teach, coach, or mentor." This can become a self-fulfilling prophecy. Your thinking drives your behavior, as we illustrated in chapter one. If you believe you don't have time, you won't.

If you think you don't have time, think again. How much time does your organization lose in recovering from preventable mistakes? How much time now is devoted to rework? How much of that time would have been saved had you and others approached each interaction purposefully and accepted accountability for providing and soliciting ongoing expectations and feedback?

One of our client CEOs, who is keenly aware of the cost of inattentive leadership, said, "I keep the Ten Principles on my desk and carry them with me. I am mindful of my need and the organization's need to coach and mentor more and to seize the opportunities to do so on a regular basis.

"A lot of people try to delegate decisions up, and you need to be conscious of that. I work very hard to help people understand what their roles are, what their capacities are, and to have confidence in them. I want them to understand that we're going to invest in the tools necessary for them to be successful and that they're going to make mistakes. They need to trust that it isn't that we wish for them to make mistakes but that we recognize that mistakes are a part of the learning process as well. How you handle that message is very, very important.

"When I slow down and use the time I have with people to truly understand them (i.e., their separate realities), I am much more conscious of the role I play with them and see the 'teachable moments' I'd missed before. Because I'm coming from curiosity much more than I ever have in the past, I am trying to expand that to say, 'Is there an opportunity here to coach?'"

Effective, accountable leaders not only mine each interaction for its potential to teach, they also make time for formal leadership development activities. In their article, "How Leaders Develop Leaders," Eli Cohen and Noel Tichy, PhD, make it clear: "For leaders to develop leaders, executives and managers must completely reexamine their most potential tool—their calendars!"

They cite the example of Roger Enrico, former chairman and CEO of PepsiCo, Inc., who helped create and deliver a ninety-day leadership program for the company. Taking three months not only gave participants the time they needed to apply the lessons he had to offer, but it also demonstrated the company's commitment to their long-term success.

Formal leadership development programs, when well constructed and managed, bring long-lasting benefits to a company. They can inspire a level of buy-in and create a language of accountability that strengthens the organization for the long-haul.

There is no either/or, however. Without formal leadership development, it is difficult, at best, to hold on to talented leaders. Without day-to-day teaching, coaching, and mentoring, the benefits of the formal program cannot be sustained over time.

So what tools can we use to provide the timely and effective feedback that cultivates leaders? As far as we have come in electronic communications technology (which I love, by the way), I don't think we have ever developed a tool more valuable than "management by walking around" (MBWA). Professor Albert Mehrabian has reported that 93 percent of the impact of a communicated message is nonverbal. The power of the face-to-face interaction is overwhelming, particularly when stacked up against that of e-mail.

There is no more powerful way to teach, coach, and mentor and no more effective way to inspire discretionary effort than to be present—physically, intellectually, and emotionally—for those we lead.

The key point to take from this principle is that each leader, manager, or supervisor has many interactions with staff, superiors, and customers every day. Each of these interactions is an opportunity to teach, coach, and mentor. To be successful at this, leaders must first create realistic expectations related to the length of planned interactions (such as meetings and workshops), and stick to them. For example, because there is often no meeting agenda or it is nonspecific or people are allowed to stray from the agenda, valuable time is lost that could be used for teaching, coaching, and mentoring—not to mention time that could be used to review action items from the meeting and to do other, more productive tasks. The previous nine principles are designed to help leaders live Principle Ten.

Accountable leadership requires not only addressing the tasks to which your team is assigned but cultivating the leadership potential in its members. It's work that will build for the future of the organization. When we teach, coach, and mentor humanistically, we are providing the foundation for a succession plan that will allow the company to grow and succeed according to its values.

Principle Ten Review: Teach, coach, and mentor—spend at least half of your time developing others.

- When you lead with intention, when you bring the previous nine principles to every interaction or task, you will find that you are already spending not 50 percent but 100 percent of your time teaching, coaching, and mentoring.

- As a teacher, you impart your knowledge, your wisdom, and your experience to others.
- As a coach, you are prepared to instruct, direct, and even prompt others to shift focus, to point them in a direction that will be more useful to them.
- As a mentor, you are an experienced guide who can help those who are less experienced.
- If we hope to lead effectively, we must be prepared to offer not only constructive feedback but praise—we must celebrate achievement (remember the Four-to-One Rule).
- Effective, accountable leaders not only mine each interaction for its potential to teach, but they also make time for formal leadership development activities.

Teach, Coach, and Mentor—Spend at least Half of Your Time Developing Others: Personal Reflection

Think about the best boss you have ever had, the leader for whom you most often volunteered your best work (i.e., discretionary effort).

1. What was it about his/her leadership that inspired your confidence?

    _____
    _____
    _____
    _____

2. How often did s/he teach, coach, and/or mentor you? How did s/he do it? What was the impact?

    _____
    _____
    _____
    _____

Now think about yourself as a leader:

3. Do you spend at least 50 percent of your time teaching, coaching, and mentoring those on your team? Why or why not? What is the impact of this on your work relationships and results?

    _____
    _____
    _____
    _____

4. If you need to increase the amount of time you spend teaching, coaching, and mentoring, how will you accomplish this? What will it take for you to become a great leader?

    _____
    _____
    _____
    _____

Be accountable now!

Conclusion

Remember, It's about Progress, Not Perfection!

. . . .

"Perfect is the enemy of good."

Voltaire

"Behold the turtle. He makes progress only when he sticks his neck out."

James Bryant Conan

"There is no such thing as a perfect leader either in the past or present. If there is one, he is only pretending, like a pig inserting scallions into its nose in an effort to look like an elephant."

Liu Shao-chi

So let's review the Ten Principles you've learned. You are going to be in the moment for your coworkers and loved ones. You will be authentic and humanistic with your colleagues and family. You will be accountable and volunteer discretionary effort constantly. You will respond with curiosity rather than judgment and accept the separate reality of the other person. You will be prepared to have courageous conversations when needed, and you will be highly skilled at delivering performance expectations and feedback. As an accountable leader, you will be prepared to teach, coach, and mentor in your human interactions. All in all, you are learning to put the Ten Principles to good use in your professional and personal relationships.

But wait—how kindly do you treat yourself? Do you slow down to be gentle with yourself, acknowledging the beliefs that have driven your behavior and accepting your own imperfections? Do you celebrate your achievements? Do you give yourself room to grow?

Too many of us reach leadership positions because we charge ahead toward perfection—often at our own expense. That pace denies us the opportunity to appreciate and celebrate what is good about ourselves, including the progress we have made. It's an attitude that costs us, robbing us of real happiness.

Given its importance, what follows is worth repeating. You may recall some of the content from earlier in the book. If you had to put a percentage on the number of things that are working well in your professional and personal life combined, what would it be? Over the years, I've asked hundreds of executives this question. Thankfully, the overwhelming majority of them have responded with an answer that has been at least 80 percent. In fact, many have said that 90–95 percent of the things in their lives were working well.

The next question I ask is this: "So, given your answer to the first question, where do you focus most of your personal attention and energy at work?" Without fail, the majority of executives/leaders who are new to the Ten Principles of Personal Leadership respond by saying that they devote almost all of their attention and energy (mental, emotional, and physical) to the 20 percent or less that could be working better—typically, to the exclusion of the 80 percent or more that is working well. When those leaders are asked, "In the workplace, what impact does this 'narrow leadership perspective' have on creating an organizational culture where people want to take risks, volunteer discretionary effort, have courageous conversations, behave accountably, etc.?," they often pause.

Typically, before long, a challenging and defensive tone can be detected in the voices of some leaders in the audience as they point out that they are "driven to succeed, to obtain perfection" in all that they do, that they have been conditioned to focus only on the 20 percent (i.e., what's wrong), and that's why they get paid the big bucks. They chide us that "the pursuit of excellence" through continuous improvement is what it's all about.

Let's be clear—we're all for continuous improvement and progress. In any improvement process, I believe in encouraging people to try out new behaviors that will produce better results, and to continuously learn from feedback and from making mistakes. Yes, I assume that people will make mistakes as they develop and grow. It is in discovering that we can learn from our mistakes that we become more resilient and successful.

Leaders who focus all of their attention and energy on the 20 percent of things that are broken—some might call this a perfectionist model—**often stifle the shaping of a culture that values continuous learning and improvement and strengthens innovation and resilience.** When we celebrate and leverage the 80 percent of things that are working well while we address the 20 percent that could be improved, we can be humanistic. We can maintain perspective (i.e., be focused on the big picture—the 100 percent, not just the 20 percent or the 80 percent) as we lead organizations and the people in them.

At the end of the day, **accountable leaders shape desired behaviors and results (i.e., high performance) by encouraging personal growth and development and by using positive reinforcement in the process.** Remember the Four-to-One Rule: To stay motivated, over time the average employee needs to hear four times as many pieces of appreciative feedback as constructive feedback. In an organization run by perfectionists, this ratio is often 1:10 or worse.

In an organization where leaders focus exclusively on the 20 percent, we often encounter what we will call a fear-based culture—one in which people are used to only hearing about failures and only hearing criticism. The resulting impact is that employees fear making mistakes. They avoid taking accountability, making decisions, and taking risks. They come to resent rather than trust leadership, and they refuse to volunteer discretionary effort. Obviously, these cultural traits act as barriers, not enablers, to continuous improvement, excellence, and sustainable growth.

This phenomenon holds true for families as well as for organizations. If, as a parent or spouse, I focus only on the things that are not going well, it's as if those are the seeds that I choose to water. The faults I focus on grow right before my eyes, until they are all I can see in my spouse and children and in myself as a member of the family.

In my own case, it was that voice in my head, which I've attributed to my dad, telling me that I wasn't good enough. I've seen this pattern repeat in watching my sons mature. My eldest son is married now, and I see him struggle with the same script. Just as I have done, he loses patience when things aren't exactly the way he'd like them to be. He sees this in himself and is working on being more accepting and less demanding.

He will do this. If I can change, I know he can too.

After years of applying the Ten Principles, I continue to learn to be more comfortable making mistakes—to acknowledge them, to learn from them, and to work for continuous improvement. I am fully conscious that my alternative is a kind of doom loop, spiraling—not upward toward perfection but downward toward misery and guilt. I've learned to accept things not being perfect in my house. I have lived with three people who have different standards than I have. Is demanding my standard of perfection and proving myself right more important than showing them that I love them? Of course not. However, per Principle Nine, it is important to negotiate and agree upon expectations and then hold family members accountable for meeting them.

Each of us has the power to escape our learned behaviors, to break free of the habits that have become barriers to our own happiness. I remind myself that the punishing voice in my head is something that I *choose* to listen to, that I choose to believe. As I said before, my father was a good man whose behavior made sense to him based on his upbringing; I know now that he was doing what he thought was best for me and doing it from a place of love. The fact that the thought *I'm not good enough; I must be perfect* has echoed in my mind for most of my life doesn't mean that it is true. I can have a courageous conversation with myself. I can challenge the premise that only perfect is acceptable. I can choose to see the good in myself, to water those seeds and see them grow. I can choose to forgive my imperfections. This is solely up to me; it is my accountability. I need to own it and change it.

It takes a kind of gentleness with my thoughts, and it takes practice. I have learned to hold these thoughts and beliefs lightly and to look at them closely. I ask myself, "Does this belief serve me well?" If the answer is no, I can reject that belief. With time, the behavior it once inspired will end. By understanding and internalizing that my thoughts and beliefs drive my behavior, I am ready and able to challenge and change them.

I can find that awareness and gentleness when I keep myself in the moment. I have learned, with practice, to recognize an old, negative belief as it's coming toward me. I recognize when I'm feeling sad, angry, or frustrated. I recognize these feelings and the impact that an old belief is about to have, and I head it off with purposeful action. I don't just react. I have the awareness to pause and choose my response to what is happening around me.

As you work with these principles in your own life, **remember that progress is what matters.** In this vein, please don't use the principles as weapons against yourself or others—use them in the spirit of love. Focus on the things that are going well, the improvements you and others are making, and those will be the seeds that will grow.

When we take the time to choose acceptance and forgiveness of ourselves and others, we become more accountable and discover greater happiness. The Ten Principles of Personal Leadership are powerful tools to help us on this journey. They have helped me accept and embrace my past and forgive those I used to blame for my unhappiness, including my parents and myself. As a result, I now experience happiness beyond what I ever imagined was possible. For this, I am extremely grateful to God and my family.

Remember: "Most folks are about as happy as they make up their minds to be" (Abraham Lincoln).

Afterword

by

Maureen McNeill

"If your mind gives way to anger, then even if the world is peaceful and comfortable, peace of mind will elude you."

The Dalai Lama

About two-thirds of the way into this project, life came at my family fast when my husband was diagnosed with cancer. It's in stage four, meaning that the cancer has invaded more than one organ and that the goal is not cure but remission. Living, for us, has a whole new, more immediate meaning.

For me, almost as much as for Mark Sasscer, this book is a labor of love. We both have full-time lives, so this is the thing we do early on weekend mornings, because we believe in the Ten Principles. When I told Mark about my husband's illness, he immediately and generously offered to free me from responsibility for the book. My decision to keep working may have been borne of stubbornness, but it has been a blessing. For me, the Ten Principles are like medicine.

Since I learned about the Ten Principles not long after working with Mark on *The Change Agent*, I embraced them. I work to use them—the words themselves—to guide my actions. When I stray, my daughter calls me on it: "Real curious, Mom. Not judgmental at all!" (We're working on the sarcasm, but my family values the concepts.)

I've brought the Ten Principles to work—I'm the director of development for the nonprofit Coastal Hospice—and we have established a leadership group, which we call Change Agents. Together we, as leaders in the organization, are working through the principles one at a time. We meet more frequently in coaching trios to help one another stay on track. This year, when Coastal Hospice signed on with a consultant to improve our quality of care while more closely guarding our resources, the Ten Principles took on new relevance.

You see, hospice workers have nearly unyielding compassion for our patients and families, but we can forget to treat one another as kindly. In the process of creating a culture of authenticity and humanism, of respecting and leveraging separate realities, we were able to introduce a new set of norms for time management and caseloads into a principle of accountability. We have new, clearly stated expectations of one another, and as an organization and as colleagues, we are much better for it.

When I said the Ten Principles have been like medicine, though, I wasn't talking about work. There is nothing like my husband's diagnosis to pull your life into sharp focus. Things that once seemed important are revealed to be trivial. That isn't always a good thing, but because I've been working with the principles, I have become better at pausing before I respond. I'm no saint, and I am grateful to know that progress and not perfection is the goal, but I have new access to peace of mind. I am a better wife and parent. I believe I am a better person.

As it happens, around the same time that we began work on this book I had begun reading books by His Holiness the Dalai Lama. For me, the two work hand in hand. Both are built on a fundamental principle of being present in the moment. Together, these two influences have opened the way to profound happiness.

Even as my life takes this new path with all of its challenges, I am grateful to have found that I can choose my steps with love.

Author's note: Prior to going to press, Maureen's husband lost his battle with cancer.

Bibliography

American Psychological Association. "The Road to Resilience." American Psychological Association. www.apahelpcenter.org/featuredtopics/feature.php?=6.

Carlson, Richard, and Joseph Bailey. *Slowing Down to the Speed of Life: How to Create a More Peaceful Simpler Life from the Inside Out.* New York: HarperCollins, 1997.

Cohen, Eli, and Noel Tichy. "How Leaders Develop Leaders." *Training and Development Magazine* 51 (1997).

Cook, John. *The Book of Positive Quotations.* Minneapolis: Fairview Press, 1997.

Daniels, Aubrey C. *Bringing Out the Best in People: How to Apply the Astonishing Power of Positive Reinforcement.* New York: McGraw-Hill, 2000.

Mehrabian, Albert. *Silent Messages: Implicit Communication of Emotions and Attitudes.* Belmont, CA: Wadsworth, 1980.

Society of Human Resource Management. "Salaries as a Percentage of Operating Expense." Society of Human Resource Management. www.shrm.org/Research/Articles/Articles/Pages/MetricoftheMonthSalariesasPercentageofOperatingExpenses.aspx Accessed 11/1/08.

Wagner, Rodd, and James Harter *12: The Elements of Great Managing.* New York: Gallup Press, 2006.

Welch, Jack. *Jack: Straight from the Gut*, New York: Warner Books, 2001.

Mark Sasscer is the founder and CEO of LeadQuest Consulting, Inc., an international leadership consulting and training firm. He holds an MS in organizational development from the American University, a BS in mathematics from Towson University, and is the author of The Change Agent. He lives in Maryland with his wife, Cheryl.

Printed in the United States
By Bookmasters